TWO STRIKES

AND

NOT OUT

The Story of George Bigelow
and the Sinking of the
SS Leopoldville

By

Larry Simotes

Copyright © Larry Simotes 2017

Acknowledgements

To my loving father who made me the man I am today. I miss you every day pops.

To my beautiful mother, my guiding angel who taught me to see all that is good in life.

And finally, to all the brave and courageous men who have served and died for our country.

PROLOGUE

It was Christmas Eve and bitterly cold in the English Channel. The sky was moonless and starless, suffocatingly dark. The icy water closed over the soldier's head as he was sucked down into the inky blackness for the third time. He felt his lungs aching to breathe and he knew this was it. The agony and pressure became unbearable as the roiling darkness swallowed him. He tried to move his arms but it felt as if they were pinned to his sides by an invisible force, pushing him, squeezing the life out of him. He was only twenty years old, was this going to be the end? Then he saw a light, an impossible light in all that cold dark water. He couldn't tell if his eyes were open or closed, he couldn't tell which way was up and which way down, but there was a light. The vision cleared a bit and he could tell it was in the shape of a nine-inch television screen. And she was smiling at him from the screen; his wife, Betty, three months pregnant with their child. She reached out her hand and he felt her strength. He yearned for her. It was as if time was completely suspended, he suddenly felt warm and safe, here in the darkness with her; with them. All at once he knew it would be a son and that son would grow to be an amazing man. George Bigelow smiled to himself and was at peace. Then, miraculously he was rising, being pushed out of the water by the churning waves as the SS Leopoldville sunk nearby. And all at once he breached the surface and felt the slap of the icy cold air on his cheeks. He could hear men screaming all around him, but in that moment, he knew the joy of being born again, being saved inexplicably to fight another day.

CHAPTER ONE
THE COFFEE SHOP

It was sometime in January, 2016, and my father had been gone for over a year and a half. Though he was 80 years old at the time, not only did I still miss him even today, but I was also having a very difficult time accepting that he was gone. Obviously, the pain of handling the loss of my father was merely the consequence of the deep love I had for him, but it was also due to the fact that I had started writing a book about my father's life two years before he was sick, and completed it a few months after he had passed. It broke my heart that he never saw "Forgotten Father" completed, and to say the least, at this time in my life I had zero interest in writing another book.

During the time my father took ill, my wife Lisa and I had just located to the sunshine state of Florida as our full-time place to live. This turned out to be a tremendous move for us since we had never been out of the Midwest our entire lives and saying goodbye to Old Man Winter was an easy decision. With no previous plans or any special place marked on the map, we found ourselves landing a home on the beautiful waters of Sarasota Bay, Florida. Though the house itself was a complete disaster, it was still on the water which granted us a place to boat, fish or just sit and view all the beauty of the bay. The sights and sounds that came from our backyard were truly special. There was something really therapeutic about watching the palm trees bend and whistle from a gulf breeze sweeping inland. Or when the tide would rise, listening to the bay waters crashing in against its shore with a rhythmic melody that only nature could have created. Then there was my favorite time; the night. Sitting outside on a clear night staring up at the stars as they glistened against the night sky, I would always ask myself the same question over and over. What is life? This was the place where I would find myself doing some of my best writing. It was also a place that was at times so peaceful, so serene, and so magical, I would often find myself writing well into the night and early into the next morning.

Now, living on the water is maybe one of the greatest things anybody could ever wish for, but many things make up a great place to live. As for my wife Lisa, after our home, friends and a good tennis club, it had to be a great coffee shop with friendly waitresses, which she eventually found in Peach's Restaurant a few blocks from our home.

Now you may ask what does a tennis club and a coffee shop have to do with this story? Well, the tennis club has absolutely nothing to do with this story. But the Peach's coffee shop has everything to do with this great story about a great man. It is where my story begins.

One day, my beautiful wife, after arriving home from Peach's, enthusiastically began telling me how she had met this 92-year-old WWII veteran. Lisa wasn't much to talk or say a whole lot, but on this day she described this old fellow as one of the cutest, nicest and most interesting men she had ever met. Personally, during my youth and even into adulthood, I always had a fondness for older people, finding them so very interesting. I could sit with them at times for hours just listening to all their stories and wisdoms of life. However, with respect to all seniors and their lives, this was not just your ordinary senior, this was a WWII veteran. What sparked my interest even more was knowing it was likely that over 99% of these brave men were now gone and with only around 500,000 out of the 16 million still with us, they were sadly dying off at a pace of 492 a day. They were known by all as our last great American generation! And truly they were.

Lisa described this fellow as a little man standing around 5 feet 9 inches tall and if lucky, 140 pounds when soaking wet. His frame matched his size though his arms and legs were not that of a 92-year-old man. In his right hand, he maneuvered a dark cherry cane to help him navigate his way around. It was easy to see that before the use of this cane he likely walked more erect and stood a couple of inches taller. When walking, he would lean forward, likely due to so many years of the gravity of life pushing down upon his fragile shoulders. On his face were these thin wire rim glasses that looked as old as he was with the gold-plated coating peeling off its frame. Remarkably, the face of this 92-year-old man looked as smooth and soft as a baby's bottom. Lisa couldn't believe his speech was as clear as his inner thoughts and while she sat there sharing conversation with this WWII hero, it felt like she was sitting across from a college professor lecturing at Harvard. Yet, Lisa told me what really made him special was when he wasn't talking seriously, he had an extremely funny sense of humor matched only by a one-of-a-kind, not-to-be-duplicated laugh. With all the special traits that this WWII war vet possessed, more important than all of this, Lisa expressed to me he was one of the sweetest men she had ever met. His name was George Edward Bigelow.

A few days had passed since Lisa had mentioned meeting George Bigelow, but one morning while I was having breakfast with her, I had the good fortune of meeting him myself for the first time. So on this one supreme morning, fate had granted me an opportunity to just sit and listen to this special man. And as I sat there, it hit me he was exactly as Lisa had described him, yet much more!

As we sat there eating our breakfast I asked George about some of his memories of his experiences of the war. Though I graduated with a major in History, one that I had not put to any good use for over thirty years, I had some knowledge of the war but still found myself weighing in on his every word this man was willing to share with me. I became completely spellbound by him.

George went into vivid detail describing to Lisa and myself the story of the sinking of the SS Leopoldville and its crew that was making its way across the English Channel to the beaches of Cherbourg, France. Right below Cherbourg were the beaches of Normandy where many thousands of United States soldiers perished to the hands of the Germans. I must confess, it was quite an extraordinary story to say the least. Also, my other confession was I was embarrassed to admit that through my history studies, I had no memory or knowledge of the SS Leopoldville sinking. I later discovered that this may have been due to the whole thing being covered up, and that the soldiers who had survived had been ordered not to talk about it to the press at the risk of having their benefits cancelled. One could say these men were cheated out of their history.

As we finished our breakfast we picked up George's tab, said our goodbyes and went on our way. That was basically the end of the story — or so I thought!

CHAPTER TWO

THE PARTY

Several weeks had passed since I had last seen George and even though Lisa and I had discussed him a few times since that morning at breakfast, we really never had a chance to sit and talk to him any further about his life. Still, as fate would have it, one night while hosting a party for family and friends (tennis friends) at our home, it hit us to invite George and our new friend, Juanita. Juanita was an amazing 84-year-old woman that I met on the airplane during one of my flights back to Illinois to spend time with my ill father.

On the night of the party the old-fashioned gentleman, George, came dressed in black slacks, beige shirt and sporting a brown tie and as we introduced George to everyone, all there just loved him.

Whether by luck, fate or against all odds, Lisa sat him next to her mother Joanne hoping that maybe lightning would strike, enticing the two to become friends; platonic friends of course! Unfortunately, George with all his charm and class didn't have much success in getting Joanne to engage in much conversation. This had much less to do with George and everything to do with Lisa's mom. You see, Joanne had lost the only man she had ever known and loved around 15 years ago and not once did she ever think of another man let alone look for another. From the time they met in high school, married and produced nine children (a good practicing Catholic with obviously bad rhythm), he was from the very beginning her soul mate and she his. During the time I courted Lisa, I never saw him once disrespect her or even raise his voice to her; at least not in public. As his prospective son-in-law, at times I wondered if he was purposely exhibiting to me the proper way to treat and respect your wife. If I am true to myself, he indeed set an extremely high standard for me and many others to reach. Still, whether I would end up marrying his daughter or not, he became in my eyes one of the greatest men that I had ever had the pleasure to have known. And after the great fortune of marrying Lisa, my only regret is that we weren't blessed with more time with him.

So now one can easily understand why after the death of Richard (Casey) Thompson Joanne never moved on to find another man.

Later that night after everyone had left the party, something possessed me to turn on my computer to explore George's story of the sinking of the SS Leopoldville. Scrolling through the details of this horrible disaster, I began to uncover the history without ever realizing the significance of the many twists and turns this story would later take on. So many mistakes, so many failures, so much bad fate causing so many Americans to grievously perish in the depths of the English Channel. I was enthralled, and also somewhat horrified at what I read. Strangely enough though, over the next few weeks, I honestly didn't give much thought to George's story after the party that night. That was, at least, not until this one particular day.

It had been about three weeks after George attended our party and up until that time I had no contact with him of any sort. However, this was going to all change the day Lisa called me to meet her for coffee down at Peach's restaurant. Though I was running late to another engagement when her phone rang that day, I decided to take her up on her invitation.

After finishing our breakfast, Lisa couldn't stay long since she was running late herself for a tennis match so I found myself following her footsteps out the front door that day. However, call it luck, fate or divine intervention as I reached to open the door, out of the corner of my eye I spotted George Bigelow in a booth sitting by himself. I told Lisa to go ahead of me as I preceded to George.

As I got up to his booth I asked, "George, how would you like to have some company?"

He smiled and just responded, "Sure." I took my seat, ordered a cup of tea as my inner spirit moved me to start inquiring about the life of the WWII Veteran. Sitting with him exchanging thoughts made it easy for me to understand there was not only a gentleness to this man, but when he spoke, he was truly genuine.

George and I sat there for almost an hour that day as he elegantly spoke about his life. Though I was mostly interested in talking to him about the sinking of the SS Leopoldville and the war, destiny led us into talking about more of his life. For a person who sometimes loves to hear myself talk, I knew my role was to just sit there and listen.

When our time was up, something inside of my heart and soul told me his story would be one that would be inspirational and moving to many. So I turned to George, expressing to him how proud and honored I would be if he would allow me write a book about his life. At that second, his chin sunk, his hands began to softly shake as he sat there in a cold silence not saying a word. I didn't know if he felt I wasn't really qualified to write his story only having written one book in my entire life and didn't really want to hurt me in telling me so. If this was not the reason, my only other thought was maybe there were things in his past he felt were just best left alone.

Luckily for me, after a couple of seconds had passed, George just smiled and said "I don't know if my life is worth telling, Larry."

Feeling his sincerity, I rebutted, "George, you have a very interesting story that needs to be told. I just hope I can rightly tell it"

Over the next month George and I would meet to have breakfast two or three days a week at Peach's. Most customers already knew of this sweetheart of a man, however, during our meetings at the coffee shop each day, customers would eavesdrop to learn just a little more each day about this war hero. It was now May and spring would be calling for George to head back home to Ann Arbor, Michigan. This would be my last week with him until we met again in October so I had a big job in front of me gathering information about his life for my book.

Strangely, on the last day we met, I was informed an article was published in our local newspaper about my own father's life and my book 'Forgotten Father,' telling his story. As his son, I was so proud that this acknowledgment about my father's truly fascinating life was written. Unfortunately for me though, each time I read my father's article it only brought me to tears. My tears were obviously for the loss of my father and the pain that went with missing him every day. But there was also the inner guilt that came from not finishing the book while he was alive. Though not completely finished upon his death, the least I could have done was read to him the chapters I had finished while he was still with me. I am not saying he wasn't proud knowing I was writing about his life because he was—very much indeed. Yet, reading it to him would have been my way of telling him in my words how proud I was to be his son and him as my father.

On the day I saw my father's story in my hometown newspaper, I also by good fate was meeting George for coffee. At breakfast, George told me that for the last fifty years he has ordered the same breakfast every day, consisting of two eggs over easy, bacon, hash browns and toast. Sometimes he would shake things up and have pancakes, but this was his meal of champions. As for me, watching this 92-year-old stud munch down on what I would call a heart attack meal, I ordered a bowl of oatmeal.

As with every time we met, George was his good spirited self, never bothered by me quizzing him about his life. However, on the last day when I handed him my father's article from back home to read, he became unusually quiet. I didn't know what to expect, nor did I ask him. A 92-year-old man doesn't need to have anyone question his feelings or inner thoughts. After finishing our breakfast and my interview now over, we both got up, I paid the bill and as always, with his trusty cane in his right hand, I escorted him to his car.

As we made our way across the parking lot and to his car, George suddenly stopped, turned to me and said, "Larry, why are you working so hard on this?" At first I was a little taken back by his question. It was hard for me to understand why he would ask this of me after all he had been through.

So, like I have always done, whether in the right or in the wrong, I just answered what was true to my heart. "George, it's a great story about a great man." I responded.

"Ah, you don't have to say that," he blurted back.

I paused for a second, then replied, "George, your life is a tremendous story that I am honored to tell. But to be completely honest with you, there is another reason I need to give your book my best effort in completing." I then put my right arm around his frail rounded shoulders and with a small crackle in my voice I whispered, "I need to finish it while you are still with us. It is something that I didn't accomplish for my own father."

As George slowly walked over to get into his car, we embraced one another one last time. With both my arms now embracing this man among men, it felt as if I was hugging my own father. And though not for sure, I saw a tear roll from his eye. One that would only be matched by my own.

CHAPTER THREE

NATIONAL GEOGRAPHIC

O n this day when we both felt we were finished with our goodbyes, he hesitated before dropping his butt into his 2003 maroon Buick Century, turned to me out of the blue and asked, "Larry, have you ever watched the story of the sinking of the SS Leopoldville on PBS and National Geographic channel?"

I wish I could have responded with a yes, but since I hadn't I politely answered "No, I haven't George why do you ask?"

Standing there beside his car in the parking lot of our local Peach's with his cane holding him up he proudly began telling me that ten years ago National Geographic with PBS had called him about doing a TV documentary about the sinking of the SS Leopoldville, and had offered an all-expenses paid trip to revisit the site in the English Channel where the ship had gone down.

"Larry," now putting his hand on my shoulder, he said, "tragically, many men who fell into the sea that night felt they had beaten death since they had their May West life preservers on, but none of them ever had a clue that within only a few minutes the cold sea decided their fate, taking their lives."

George, not one to turn down an adventurous journey or a free trip told me he had quickly accepted Nat Geo's offer to go back to the Leopoldville's graveyard on one condition, that his daughter Robin could make the trip with him. National Geographic had agreed and off they went to Cherbourg, France.

After arriving in Paris, George and Robin were promptly bussed to Cherbourg where the next morning the two found themselves making introductions to the entire PBS camera crew, before being escorted aboard a huge fifty-foot sea vessel. The ship set the co-ordinates to head out to the exact location where the

Leopoldville had lain for over sixty years deep at the bottom of the English Channel. The famous author, Clive Cussler, had taken an expedition out in 1984 and had located the sunken wreck. Cussler dedicated his 1986 book *Cyclops* to the disaster and to the good men that lost their lives there. It was twenty-five years later now and George and the film crew were heading out to that very location, 49 44 40. 01 36 40 on the sea map.

As the vessel made its five-mile journey from the shores of Cherbourg, France, George shared with me that with every mile the sea vessel traveled to the location, his head was filled with the ungodly images of the many dead men floating in the sea all around him. And yet here he was, heading to where the SS Leopoldville had taken a hit from the German U-486 torpedo to sink into the dark sea on that horrible Christmas Eve in 1944; this monstrous location where George would now be asked to recall his story of one of the worst losses of life at sea in American history.

With the cameras now staring George straight in the face the production manager of the film crew walked over and asked, "George are you ready to take all of us back to that night?"

George took his time before responding, then calmly said, "You know it's been a long time since that night when so many men died without their stories ever being told. Maybe this will help the families of those who never made their way out of the sea that night alive."

It would take around four or five hours for the film crew and George to review the underwater video of the wreckage as he told his story of that tragic night. And even though it was a difficult task for him to discuss the sinking, having his loving daughter Robin at his side during the entire filming kept him as cool as a cucumber...well, almost.

Now with the filming complete, the crew presented George with a beautiful bouquet of red roses to toss into the sea, giving tribute to all the fallen men that night. However, when the crew captain signaled George to toss the roses overboard, still holding the roses in his hand while leaning against the ship's rail staring into the sea, he felt his right hand tightly grasping the rail of the vessel exactly as he had done on that dreadful night; the night the Leopoldville began to list to starboard, throwing him backwards into the frigid waters. As he looked down into the English Channel waters his mind sailed him back to that cold dreadful night. Staring deep into these waters he saw himself standing on the Leopoldville's deck grabbing onto its rail, squeezing it with all his God-given strength to keep himself from being drawn down with the ship's suction to the bottom of the ocean floor. But this would prove futile as his grip was ripped away from the rails of the ship, sending him down into the utter darkness of the sea.

It all came flooding back now as he stood there so many decades later looking down at the very spot where it happened. It was surreal. George remembered descending, deeper and deeper to the bottom of the sea, he remembered how he had furiously used his arms like a hummingbird flapping its wings to try and keep himself from plummeting into the depths . The time had come to put his life in God's hands and that is exactly what he did. With his eyes closed and no longer able to hold his last breath, his mouth opened allowing the sea water to fill his lungs. Unconsciousness would now follow, but while he was suspended deep in the dark, cold sea, hovering between life and death, he would find himself looking into a nine-inch black and white TV. It would be a screen taking him back to his youth, and his first love.

CHAPTER FOUR

LEWISTOWN AND JAMES AND ELLA BIGELOW

George Edward Bigelow was born on March 14th, 1924 in a typical small, mid-eastern town in Lewistown, Pennsylvania located in Mifflin County. It lies along the Juanita River, 61 miles (98km) northwest of Harrisburg. It was settled in 1790 and by 1900 had a population of 4,451. The borough was incorporated in 1795 and was named for William "Bill" Lewis, a Quaker and a member of the legislature.

During the late 19th century, Mifflin County became a crossroads of the Commonwealth. Located near the geographic center of the state, it became a crossroad hub for traffic moving in every direction. Early roads crisscrossed the region, but it was the construction of the Pennsylvania Canal and the railroads that made Lewistown boom. Sadly, with more advanced travel and the decay of the canal system, Mifflin County would later lose its mark as a transportation hub.

One note of historical interest would stamp Lewistown in the history books. During the Civil War on April 16th, 1861, Lewistown sent its Logan Guards, a militia group originally formed in 1858, to Washington, D.C. for its defense. They were one of only five companies, all recruited in Pennsylvania, to share the honor of being the first U.S. troops sent to the capital. At the intersection of Main and Market streets in Lewistown, stands the Monument Square serving as a memorial to these men.

Though not many, there were some notably famous people that came from Lewistown, Pennsylvania. There was the 6'3", 231 pound Penn State graduate Ralph Baker, a professional football player who was drafted 38th in the third round and wore number 51 for the New York Jets from 1964-1974. He would go on to play linebacker for the Jets over the next 141 games during his eleven-season career. After his playing days were over, in 1979 he was hired as Vice Principal of the Chief Logan High School in Mifflin County. Unfortunately, due to an angry and rebellious student body, Mr. Baker and the school's head principal would be forced to resign only after one year. He did though retire as a principal of Tuscarora Junior High School in Mifflintown, Pennsylvania, in 2010. It's hard to keep down a Jets linebacker!

Another notable from Lewistown was Carl F. Barger. Barger became the President of the Pittsburgh Pirates Major League Baseball team from 1987 through 1991 and later became the first president of the Florida Marlins on July 1991. Sadly, Barger suffered an aneurysm during the MBL's Winter Meetings in 1992 in Louisville, Kentucky and would later die. On April 5th, 1993, the day that the Marlins played their first ever regular season game, in memory of Barger, the Marlins retired the number 5 to honor Barger's favorite player Jumping Joe DiMaggio, a name that George would soon come to know.

Yes, there would be a few more notables such as Julia Kasdorf; poet, El McMinn; attorney and acoustic string fingerstyle guitarist, and Carolyn Meyer; author of novels for children and young adults.

Still, before all these notables became noticed, no other person put Lewistown on the map. That is, not until the birth of our hero, George Edward Bigelow.

In the year of 1913, George's father, James William Bigelow chose Ella Jane Crownover to become his wife. Soon this union would bear five children while honoring their wedding vows for almost sixty wonderful years.

James Bigelow's appearance was a dominating one since he was a large man standing well over six feet tall and weighing over 230 pounds. However, his pride in the Bigelow name and its tradition was larger than his own stature.

Though James only had an 8th grade education, he not only trained himself in becoming a gifted electrician, but had also a keenness for making money. Whether it was buying farmland, renting homes or selling eggs, he produced revenue. Even in his later years, he purchased a local grocery store just so his first born son Fred could have a job. A job he would perform for the rest of his adult life.

James William Bigelow among all his talents, also was a very religious man whose faith and beliefs never wavered. And although he was a shrewd businessman, a strong disciplinarian and faithful supporter of the church, he made sure his kids were taught how to give back.

And James Bigelow taught by example. After the bombing of Pearl Harbor during WWII, he volunteered to work at the shipyard in Hawaii in the Central Pacific. He would pack his bags to head west from his little town of Lewiston to help his country. James Bigelow would routinely let his kids know his family was born of English descent in the late 1300s and a Bigelow had fought in every major war of the United States since. James Bigelow would be gone for almost a year working in Pearl Harbor, leaving his wife Ella and five children behind.

I could see from talking to George that as a young boy he never understood why his father had left his mother and family for such a long time, and sadly, as a ninety-year-old man, he still doesn't understand it.

Another story he told me about his father, James Bigelow, was that during the Great Depression years, local people would bring him their appliances such as toasters, washers etc. to be repaired while he never even took a cent for his services.

As the years passed and James was in late retirement, one day while getting out of his car, he took a hard fall. James would never be the same man after that fall and It was only a few years later that James Bigelow would be gone, shortly after his 77th birthday.

If James William Bigelow had been the backbone of the family, his wife Ella Jane Bigelow was the chest which the family rested their heads upon. Standing only around five feet tall, she was a beautiful looking woman with gorgeous reddish brown hair giving an elegant contrast to her crystal-blue eyes. An intelligent woman, she was not only in charge of all the duties of running the household, but she also possessed all the natural educational skills of a school teacher. She would use these skills to keep her children not only moving down the right path in school, but also following the righteous path of God's word. Ella Janie Bigelow would live to be 97 years old.

The Bigelows were the type of salt-of-the-earth people that made this country great, and their family life is what formed the characters of boys like George Bigelow, and all those other young soldiers who were going to war to defend their country. These boys had been brought up with strong values of patriotism and family, they had courage and strength of character forged by discipline that we can only wish our current generation would aspire to. Yes, they have been called the last great American generation for good reason. And George Bigelow was about to be challenged to the very core of his soul and upbringing. He was going to have to reach down very deep indeed to find the will to survive that was his heritage.

CHAPTER FIVE

FIVE CHILDREN

B aby George didn't enter this world as a large dominating figure by any means. James and Ella Bigelow had waited nine years after the birth of their first-born son, Fred Homer Bigelow, for their second child to show up. On March 14th, 1924, the long wait was over and another boy entered their lives. They would name him George Edward Bigelow. From the day of his birth, he was very small, very thin, and not very strong.

As he grew into his grade school years, his size didn't match his intelligence and wit. What else didn't help his stature as tough guys go, was due to his bad eye sight at an early age, he wore these thick, soda-pop-bottom glasses on his face. Even back in the early 1930s, that type of eyeglasses would automatically plant the word "dork" on the front of your forehead. However, like the old saying goes, "never judge a book by its cover."

Now George may not have been an Adonis in stature, but that brain in his head was for sure his biggest muscle. My own father had this old saying which he would quote to my brothers and I when we would do something stupid. "You guys have a brain like a BB in a train box car," was his quote. So, I guess if our brains were only a muscle, we would be in trouble. As for George, this scenario really didn't apply. Please let me inform you just how good of a student George Bigelow was.

During his grade school years, the school teachers had a motivational program that awarded free movie passes every month to the top student in the class. George attended so many free movies during his early school boy years that his classmates were predicting that he was destined to become a famous movie critic. Unfortunately for George, this would have been much more pleasing to his father than what George would years later grow up to be.

You see, the Bigelows had three generations of doctors that ran in their family dating back to the 17th century. With George's older brother Fred making his mark in the family grocery store, it seemed logical that George, with his brains, grades and leadership traits was a natural to go into the medical field. One could almost say James Bigelow had put all his hopes and dreams on his second son following in the family tradition of doctors. But like the great poet Robert Burns wrote, "The best-laid schemes of mice and men oft go awry."

Ok, so George was basically your good old boy. His grades were perfect and he was leader of what was called back then the "Gut Club." This was a club of boys in the neighborhood that would gather to play baseball, football and other sporting events. It was George's role to make sure the games were held on the proper dates and times and that all the equipment needed was on site. Between studying and being the leader of the Gut Club, the only day he had time to work at his father's grocery store was on Saturdays. A day he never missed unless he was really, really sick or had a crisis. He would have loved to have worked on Sunday, but the problem was in Lewistown at this time there were what were called "Blue Laws." These were basic laws that when formed together as a group meant only one thing; nothing takes place on Sunday except the worship of the Lord. In other words, attending church!

Now as perfect as George may have been, he did commit some dubious crimes. The first bad thing he would do over his parent's wishes would be to hitch hike from Lewistown to Philadelphia to watch the Philadelphia Athletics Major League Baseball team play. It's not that his parents didn't love baseball; how could they not? Baseball was America's favorite pastime and the most watched and listened to sport in the country. It was just the thought of seeing their little boy robbed, kidnapped or worse; well you know what I'm talking about, that created some uneasiness. The second dubious deed was telling a white lie rather than truly lying. Lying is never a good thing but telling a white lie is at times ok as long it doesn't hurt anybody.

One example of this was while George was in the first grade, for whatever reason, whether bad vision or possibly a phobia of clocks, the boy who grew up so smart had a hell of time telling time. So one day when he kept getting the time wrong in class, his teacher Mrs. Harding embarrassed him by ordering him to go stand in the hallway outside the classroom instructing him not to come back to class until he could walk back into class and tell her what the right time was on the hallway clock. After a few minutes passed, the pressure began mounting since he still didn't know what time was on that hallway clock that late morning. Though he had not figured out the time, he did have a keen inner sense of when the bell would be sounding off for recess and he knew it must be soon. This was going to be a huge problem because as he sat there on his little butt, all of his peers would rush over him making him feel shorter that he already was. He had to think and move fast!

Sitting there with his head between his legs feeling all was lost, he heard the sound of someone's heels clicking down the hallway against the freshly polished tile floor. As the sound grew louder and louder, through the poorly lighted corridor his eyes could make out an older student strolling in his direction. At that second the genius in him came to the forefront. As the student approached him, he took off his glasses, tucked them into his shirt pocket not to be seen, then he barked out, "Hey, could I ask you for a big favor?"

The student replied, "Yea what do you need?"

"I lost my glasses and don't see very well without them. Would you please tell me what time is on that clock on the wall?" The passing student promptly informed him that the time was 10:45. George thanked him, reached into his shirt pocket for his glasses and meticulously aligned them on his face. From here he took a deep breath, turned the doorknob to enter back into the classroom and grinning from ear to ear, he proudly walked in.

Mrs. Harding wasted no time asking him if he knew the time. George assertively responded, "It is 10:45, or as of now 10:46, Mrs. Harding."

"That's right Mr. Bigelow," Mrs. Harding confirmed. "You can go take your seat."

After that day, George never had to stand in that hallway ever again. He would also never go on to fulfill his father's dream of the second son becoming a doctor either.

Mary Ellen Bigelow, the third child, would follow George two years later. Of all the kin in the family, Mary was absolutely the spitting image of her father. She was tough, rough and had her father's drive to make a buck. She would even marry a man who had a bigger drive in making money, even more than herself. However, Mary and her husband turned out to be very successful business partners their entire lives.

Although all Bigelow children witnessed, experienced, and likely were impressed with their father's will to produce income, George on the contrary, never bought into the concept of making lots of money. This for reasons never known, would later in their lives drive a small wedge between George and his sister Mary.

Still, clone of her father or not, she was the pride and joy of her mother. A daughter's love of her mother and a mother's love for her daughter will always be undaunted.

Ernest Blair Bigelow came after Mary and was undoubtedly their father's favorite. This may have been because he was one of the hardest workers in the family. He would master the skill of a journeyman brick layer and many other construction trades. His masterfulness as a bricklayer would serve him well for his entire adult life.

Sadly, as close as Ernest and his father were, later in adulthood, Ernest chose to marry a Catholic girl against his father's wishes. This would lead to the two having a tremendous falling out.

The day that Ernest and his bride exchanged their vows was supposed to be the happiest day in the couple's lives. Instead, it would turn out to be one of Ernest worst. From that special day, his father would rarely if ever speak to his son again. This was something that brought much pain for Ernest for many years. Though it wasn't as painful as him witnessing the sadness it brought his poor mother.

Life brings us all happiness and sadness that also comes with many regrets. The fact is that there are no do-overs. So if we are lucky, we all hope to get things right the first time. Sadly, the last meaningful conversation Earnest had with his father was that day on his father's death bed. On that day he was once again his father's favorite son.

The last of the Bigelows, George's youngest brother, would be Glenn Franklin Bigelow. Up until now, the Bigelow family had been basically blessed by God with little if no hardship in their early years. But this would all change with the birth of Glenn.

Glenn just didn't show the same mental or physical advancements as the four previous children. By the time Glenn was three or four years old, it was discovered he had some form of mental retardation. I know today we don't use the term 'retarded,' but that's just what was used back then. Unfortunately, Glenn could only attend school up until the sixth grade.

Sometimes in life when things look to be at their bleakest, little things take place that allow us to find some solace. Glenn, may have been more autistic than retarded. It is just that back in those times, there was not much research, if any, on autism like there is today.

Glenn couldn't read or write, couldn't do math or many difficult daily functions. But what he could do was something that was truly incredible. Glenn could recite to you just about every major-league baseball player's statistics if he had the chance to view the back of their baseball card. And I mean just after one time! It was obvious that part of his brain was so advanced, it made him a borderline Albert Einstein when it came to recalling numbers.

After buying packages of baseball cards, Glenn would frantically rip the wrapper off, throw away the bubble gum sticker located inside and bury his head down on the cards to read the stats off the back. Whether the ball player was an established star, rookie, or just a bench warmer, he would ramble on for hours reciting his baseball facts in front of his peers. In this he was in his glory.

As Glenn grew into adulthood, he never married, never had children and he never acquired the necessary qualities to hold a job or survive on his own. But often these are the times when an angel floats down and lands on your shoulders. For Glenn, he always had this angel close by.

Ella Bigelow, the loving mother of the Bigelow family took her son in and watched over him up until he died. George shared with me that on the day Glenn passed, his mother turned to him, whispering her life was now complete. A few weeks after Glenn's passing, Ella Bigelow followed her son into heaven. She was 97.

CHAPTER SIX
FIRST LOVE

There was a beautiful young girl who attended the same high school in Lewistown, Pennsylvania as did George Bigelow, though their paths never crossed. No athletic events, no sock hops, their eyes never even met while passing each other in the hallways. At the time, this young girl resided on the far north end of Lewistown while George lived at the southern end. Still, a couple of years later, love sent cupid with his arrow pointing in their direction.

It was now March 14th, 1942 and George had just had his 18th birthday. He had now been out of high school for almost nine months and had been working at Joe the Motorists' Friend, an automotive parts store in Lewistown.

Now George's father, James, was the poster boy for the hardest working man on the entire south side of Lewistown, and he taught George that there was nothing wrong with a hard day's work. However, the problem here was that because he held the highest expectations for all of his children, James Bigelow was a difficult father to please. So when his brightest son chose not to attend college to become a doctor, choosing instead to work at an automotive parts store, James was not happy—to say the least.

There was no doubt that George was not going to make it in a career selling automotive parts and Mr. Williams, the owner of the store, knew it. Though this very sharp kid may not end up becoming a doctor like his father had planned for him, his father James wouldn't have much longer to feel his disappointment in his son. Destiny had its own plans for George. A destiny that would save many in so many ways.

George had been working at the parts store for almost nine

months since graduating from high school. It was a small company employing four or five people and since men dominated this field, only men were ever seen working there. Of course, this was all about to change the day George eyes landed on the most beautiful girl he had ever seen entering through the front office. As she walked through door of the office that day, though innocent in his behavior, George's eyes first started at the tips of her head taking in her thick, rich, auburn hair looking as soft as that of a baby mink. Then his eyes were drawn to her face, a face that had a sheen as smooth as a piece of silk. And her body was so, well, you know what I mean. Still, with all the beauty that this young girl possessed, even from afar, it was those deep blue eyes that caught George's fancy.

As George stood there in a daze, Mr. Williams called out for all of his employees to come over so he could introduce this young lady to his staff. George being the last hired, stood at the end of the line waiting his turn as the owner introduced his staff to this newcomer.

When Mr. Williams got to George, he broke the ice by saying, "This is George and like you, he is one of our newest employees. I think you both are also close to the same age."

George, with his heart pounding and his palms clammy, reached out his hand before Mr. Williams could even say her name. Standing there as stiff as a board, he spoke, "Glad to meet you, I'm George Bigelow."

The gorgeous blue-eyed young girl answered back "it's nice to meet you George. I'm Betty Gilchrist."

Six months later, on August 22nd, 1942, Betty Gilchrist would become Mrs. George Bigelow.

It was a hot sunny day when George and Betty left Grove Memorial Methodist Church on their wedding day. Unlike today, with so many people having huge weddings and receptions, there wasn't much fanfare about this day, with just a few relatives from both sides of the family and a couple of friends in attendance. Still, love is not measured by the size of a wedding party, but the size of the love in one's heart.

George and Betty would find themselves a small apartment and together they began to plan their future. One little problem was, that with both of them still working for Joe the Motorists' Friend, money was running a little scarce. However, George already had the wheels of his master plan in motion. He soon would be taking a job welding in Delaware, Virginia, while attending college at night, and taking on any side jobs that were available. When all these things had finally fallen into place, he would hopefully start to make plans for a family.

Now if you were a betting man, it would have been a really poor wager to have bet against George Bigelow's fulfilling any of his goals or dreams. This was a very smart young man with a work ethic that was maybe only second to his fathers. So it was apparent that the future of George and Betty's success was all on his shoulders. However, no matter how any of us plan our future, the crystal ball never looks the same from day to day. And so it was with George and Betty. Nine months into their marriage, something so beautiful, so perfect, so blessed entered into George and Betty's life. Betty would become pregnant.

All children born to this earth are a gift from God, though a first born is truly something really special. So, the news of Betty's pregnancy brought a joyous blessing into this couple's early marriage. Sadly, as fast as life can bring so much joy, it can take it away. And even if the foot-of-fate doesn't always squash this joy, it can surely at times press its heel heavily upon it. The footsteps that were about to squash George and Betty's dreams would soon be crunching up their path.

The day was March 14th, 1943. It was on George's 19th birthday when there was a knocking at his front door. As Betty slowly opened the door, for reasons only God may know, for some strange reason a slight cold sweat had overcome her as a six sense told her this knock was not good. Standing on her porch was a postal worker with a letter stamped 'important' from the United States government. Usually George and Betty had to walk out to retrieve their mail in the box at the end of the driveway, but not on this day. For whatever reason, whether his duty or not, the post man decided to hand deliver it. With letter in hand, as the postman gently reached out to hand the envelope to Betty, a chill instantly ran through her body as her hand reluctantly reached out to grab on to it. After the letter was now securely in her hand, she thanked the postal worker, then proceeded to stare at it as she slowly made her way back to the kitchen. On any other day a tax letter would cause a cold sweat or make one's legs buckle, unfortunately, a tax letter this was not. No, the front of this envelope had the heading the US Military stamped on the front. Betty didn't really want to open it. She knew what was inside of it. It was a draft notice requiring her husband to participate in the war—a war he only had thirty days to report to!

Now George Edward Bigelow was one tough son-of-a-gun, but when he got home after work that night and found his young bride sitting at the kitchen table in tears, a cold sadness overcame him.

Still, without showing his panic, he calmly asked, "Honey, what's wrong?" Saying nothing, his beautiful wife sat there with her folded arms acting like a pillow for her head while her hands tightly clutched the piece of paper. George calmly moved closer to see what this crumpled piece of paper was. He then gently separated Betty's fingers loosening it from Betty's grip and raised the letter up to his eyes and cautiously began to read it. Silently he moved closer to his wife, wrapping his arms around her and hugging her as tightly as he had ever hugged her in their short marriage.

That evening George and Betty cried together until there were no more napkins left to wipe their tears dry.

CHAPTER SEVEN
ON THE BUS

It had only been a week since George had received his draft notice and he was off on a bus to Fort Indiantown Gap Pennsylvania, 23 miles northeast of Harrisburg. This would be the first stop towards fighting in World War II. Here the army would give the "to be soldiers" their physicals, mental evaluations and make a decision as to what branches of the military they would be grouped in.

Now, any half-wit of a person would assume the military had this complex way of deciding if one soldier was best fitted for the Army, while another for the Air force, etc. Well, our military did have a system, it was just much simpler. George told it like this, "After all the registration was complete, they lined us all up together and proceeded to count us out...one, two, three, four; one number for each of the four branches of the military. I felt I would absolutely be tagged for the Airforce but my number sent me to the Army. This was the method in which you were sent to represent your country."

Leaving one's wife and family behind to go fight a war is something that most of us will never be able to describe let alone live through. This is what George Bigelow would be dealing with. He thought back to the day that Betty had handed him his draft notice; the look in her eyes would haunt him. He thought about his unborn baby and wondered if he would see it grow up. The military ingrained in these men that your fellow soldiers were your only family now, and you had better put all your faith in them because on the battlefield your family back home would be no use to you.

After George was sent into the army division group, something really special would happen to him, though he wouldn't really know how special until many weeks later. A soldier from Hammond, Indiana would enter his life. His name was Don Goble.

In the next 11 months, George would be shipped to Jacksonville, Florida for basic training, then eight weeks later stationed in St. Augustine, Florida, with his next stop landing him in April of 1943 at Camp Blanding, Florida for Advanced Training. This was the Army's 66th Infantry Division activated on April 14th, 1943 for engagement in Northern France. The 66th Infantry wore an insignia on their shoulder sleeve of a Black Panther in a circle outlined in red, set against an orange background with a vicious Black Panther's head symbolizing power, aggressiveness, stealth, and endurance of the 66th Infantry—and last of all, the ability to kill. This patch was designed by Nicholas Viscardi, a comic book artist who earned two Purple Hearts for wounds suffered in tank warfare while serving in the 66th Infantry Division from 1943-1945. In the Black Panther Division, soldiers mastered advanced skills in infantry, amphibious survival and physical feats such as hiking in full gear up a hill from sun up until sundown. These were just some of the training methods the military would use to prepare these men to fight, however, the biggest test the Black Panthers Division performed to demonstrate their courage would be the 'Tank Test.' Or what General Herman F. Kramer of the 66th Infantry called 'big balls' test. The test was really pretty simple. Soldiers would have to lay in a narrow ditch facing up while a US M4 Sherman Tank would drive over the men dusting the men with the dirt from its tracks. These are the men who made up the Black Panther Division. The test had a small twist to it since these men were being trained to kill Germans by General Herman who was curiously of German descent.

During these last onerous 11 months, there was one magical occurrence that had taken place. That young soldier from Hammond, Indiana that George met on his first day in Indiantown, was still at his side. It would be fair to say Don Goble and George had not only become best friends, but had become substitutes for the families they had both left behind.

Now being drafted and leaving his bride Betty while she was

carrying their three-month-old child brought much pain and tears for both of them. Still, Betty did her best to write and come visit all she could while George was still stationed in the United States. Whenever George got a three day leave he would catch a train home to be with his wife. At this time, Betty had to move in with her mother since there just wasn't enough revenue for her to support herself on her own. So often we have heard of couples living on love and this was so very true for George and Betty. But love wasn't paying the bills and when one of the lovers is many miles away you are not living on love, but on loneliness.

Each time George would have to break away from his loving wife Betty to go back, the pain was matched only by the knowing that only a year into their beautiful marriage, they would once again be hundreds of miles away far from the loving hugs that they once shared. The term "War is Hell" has been used by millions through the ages, yet, I don't think people really realize how true this is. War stands for nothing that is good. Only much pain, suffering and death.

Still, with all this sadness there was one silver lining; George's feet were still firmly planted in the United States of America. Many ocean miles from the death and destruction of the war—or so he thought.

In the next few months George would be transferred to Camp Joseph Robinson near Little Rock, Arkansas to finish his training at Camp Rucker, Alabama. In November 1944, the 66th Division would arrive at Camp Shanks, New Jersey, its final stop before being shipped overseas. Soon the 66th Division would board the George Washington on its way to England as the division was billeted in small towns and barracks at Camp Blandford in the County of Dorset on the southern coast of England.

Yes, George Bigelow was now on his way to fight, to live or to die.

CHAPTER EIGHT

SOUTHAMPTON

I t was November 14th, 1944 at Camp Shanks, New Jersey, and two people stood at the shores to see George Bigelow off to England. One, a young loving wife carrying George's baby while the other, a mother seeing her young son looking much more like a man than the young boy she knew. Either way, Betty Bigelow and Ella Bigelow soaked their handkerchiefs this day, mopping up the tears, knowing they might not see their beloved George again.

After giving his last kisses and hugs to Betty and his mother, George reluctantly boarded the ship, saying his last goodbyes to the most precious women in his life. Since he was well trained in the Black Panther Division and a highly-touted staff sergeant, he was conditioned not to show any kind of weakness at his departure. Still, with all the training the army had ever given him, there's no special training for the pain of leaving one's loved ones behind. Yet, with all the tears and sadness, there was one silver lining; George's best friend, Don Goble, was still at his side. Conflicting emotions churned inside all the boys in the lines that day, inching closer with every step to the war that was both so exciting and yet so dreadful. These boys were mostly still teenagers, who only a few weeks ago might have been smashing their bats into baseballs and running for all they were worth around a field with their friends in the stands egging them on, and soon they might be literally running for their lives.

Upon arriving at Southampton, England, George would receive his last few weeks of special ops training before stepping on the SS Leopoldville, a Belgian cruise liner that had been converted to a troop ship, to set sail across the English Channel for Cherbourg, France. After months away from his loved ones and months of the finest training the U.S. Military could provide, it was now the time to go and fight for his country.

George, best friend Don Goble, and every soldier of the 66th had been enjoying their stay in Dorchester, England. Anything was better than to be called upon to kill or be killed. Yet, they fearfully waited for four weeks for the time when they would get the call to hop on a ship sailing across the English Channel to France to be deployed to Belgium to support the war in the "Battle of the Bulge." On December 16th, Hitler launched 250,000 troops against the United States 80,000 men by surprise blitzkrieg in attempt to split allied forces in northwest Europe. The United States forces were caught off guard suffering a tremendous amount of casualties. If not for Lieutenant George S. Patton's and the third army, many more lives would have been lost. Still, many soldiers were eager to join the fight since so many had friends and family fighting on the front.

Though the regiments were well prepared physically and mentally for what lay ahead of them, the famous 66th Black Panther Division had the best esprit de corps. Though a French term meaning 'the spirit of the body,' as for the 66th, it stood for comradeship, enthusiasm, and devotion to a cause among the members of a group. For George Edward Bigelow, the Black Panther Division instilled loyalty and pride deep inside of him to protect his fellow Panther even if meant the hand of death might take him.

Then at noon on December 23, 1944, orders came in from the camp in southern England that it was time to move out. The three regiments of the 66th Infantry, the 262nd, 263rd and the 264th were in separate locations since arriving in England, so soldiers needed to be quickly rounded up. The order came so fast and without warning. The Red Cross in London was commissioned to assist in rounding up the soldiers of the 66th Division, instructing them to return swiftly to camp. It was only two days before Christmas and the cooks had started preparing for the Christmas day feast. Many of these boys were still teenagers, barely on the cusp of manhood, so you can imagine their disappointment when the half-cooked Christmas dishes had to be thrown away, and duffel bags loaded, as orders came down. The soldiers had just two hours to catch the trucks transporting them to board the SS Leopoldville, bound for France.

With much apprehension, the soldiers formed at the truck pick up site but it was the Army's same old modus operandi, "hurry up and wait," with men having to wait for over five hours before the bumpy miserable ride to Southampton with empty stomachs for another five hours.

Upon arriving at the beautiful harbor town of Southampton, they were told that all boarding had hastily been halted. Whether due to a mistake or incompetence, though neither one was really acceptable, it turned out that one of the two troop ships had inadvertently loaded 2000 paratroopers and all of them needed to be removed before boarding could begin! It was chaos. Finally, after the last paratrooper was on solid ground, the men were given the go-ahead to start boarding the SS Leopoldville and her sister ship the SS Cheshire. George and his best friend Don were told to go and stand in line so they could board the Leopoldville. As George stood in line staring up at the SS Leopoldville, this colossal ship with its enormous crew waiting to board her, he felt dwarfed by its sheer size. He thought of Betty and their unborn baby, and shuddered. Standing there on the dock with Don beside him in the shadow of this colossus-of-a-ship, not knowing what fate was in store for them, their chests felt tight and emotions twisted in their gut. The fear and apprehension coming from the thousands of young inexperienced soldiers would have been palpable on the dock that night as they craned their necks up to scan the Leopoldville's awesome, looming hull.

The SS Leopoldville was 479 feet long with a 62 foot beam and a tonnage of 11,509, that had at one time been a passenger liner of the Compagnie Belge Maritime du Congo launched in 1929. Due to the war though, she was converted to a troopship to transport reinforcements to depleted forces fighting the Battle of the Bulge. Since 1940, the Leopoldville had transported over 120,000 men safely to their destinations, crossing the English Channel 24 times, never being hit by enemy fire. Her crew was impressive in making the transition from passenger service to wartime transportation of troops and supplies, and her current captain, Charles Limbor, had been in command since 1942. At 0200 (2 am) on Christmas Eve, December 24, 1944, soldiers finally began boarding.

At the docks and on the ship, after all the fiascos prior to the troops' arrival, many enlisted men waited for hours for instructions to board and where to proceed to their living quarters. One or two corporals with clipboards in their hand would ask each group what company they were in. Yet, for whatever reason which we may never know, indiscriminately the corporals assigned men of the same regiments to both ships instead of the practiced military protocol of keeping the units of soldiers all together. It was no doubt a process that made many of the men uneasy and even scared.

After many hours of standing and doing nothing, from 1:00 am, soldiers finally walked along the planks, finally setting foot on one of the troop ships. As the men arrived on deck, with no plans given to them, the soldiers once again would find themselves standing around. Many sat on wooden crates in converted cargo holds, others made good use of benches, a lucky few found make sift hammocks, while others exhausted from standing in line with the weight of heavy field gear on their backs, fell to the floor to sleep. It wouldn't take long before George knew this one-time passenger liner was not going to be taking him on a cruise vacation.

As a well-trained staff sergeant, he stood witnessing as troops hastily and without organization began boarding the ship with 2223 reinforcements from the 262nd and 264th Regiments, 66th Infantry Division. He watched as the soldiers' regimental command structure was fragmented by loading troops as they arrived rather than their units. Regiments were mixed together and companies were spilt, platoons found themselves distributed throughout the 479ft Leopoldville, making communication almost impossible between the men and their captains. With so much chaos, confusion and overcrowding, the men felt like sardines in a tin can. This was not the best therapy for a soldier's morale, especially for those who were soon going to fight, and likely many would die. Still, as

George stood there looking down from the deck of the ship watching all the crazy confusion, his eyes suddenly became drawn to much more troublesome issues. First, he noticed so few troops were participating in the poorly supervised lifeboat training procedure as the ship started its departure from Southampton. Even George himself never heard the call for Infantrymen to organize together for the boat drill, which was later rumored to have been due to the loud speakers malfunctioning in some of the holds. However, the real reason for so much lack of organization was also because so many group leaders were, from the beginning, separated from their regiments. As a staff sergeant, the thing George knew above all was the importance of organization, instruction and command, and he was witnessing none of the above.

At 9am when the Leopoldville began its departure from the docks, as bad as the lack of troop organization may have been, something much more alarming caught George's intuition—an intuition that drew him to the area where the lifeboats and life jackets were located. Tragically, he didn't need to count them to realize there were not nearly enough for the 2,223 men aboard the ship.

Sadly, George would never have dreamed his intuition would later turn into a premonition.

CHAPTER NINE
SETTTING SAIL FOR CHERBOURG

A ny novice in the military could have told you that by the poorest of U.S. Military standards, the launching of the SS Leopoldville did not get off on the right foot, to say the least. However, with its sister ship, Cheshire, sailing along beside her, and the fact that the SS Leopoldville had lived a charmed life, never getting hit, George began to feel a little better and his uneasiness was abating. Also, it was assumed that the US military always went to great pains and took extreme measures to assure the safety of its men, so the excitement for the journey and a sense of adventure began to take over. But as the Leopoldville broke from the docks to set sail and navigated away from the safety of the port, it became apparent that the waters of the English Channel were extremely choppy, causing many of the men to become sea sick. Still, the SS Leopoldville with all the chaos, was on her way to France followed by the SS Cheshire trailing now around 200 yards behind her. The convoy set sail in a diamond formation at 0900 hours (9am) from Southampton. Due to all the German submarine activity in the area, the Leopoldville would also be escorted by the destroyers HMS Brilliant and HMS Anthony, the frigate HMS Hotham, and the French frigate Croix de Lorraine. However, even with four destroyer escorts to protect the troop ships, the German submarines had one tremendous advantage over them; the implementation of the 'Schnorchel,' a raised metal ventilation tube that enabled the submarines to draw in air, and which allowed the U-Boats to remain submerged indefinitely.

On December 18th, 1944, one such U-Boat had recently sunk the British cargo ship Silverlaurel. Fortunately, the ship and all of the 68 crew members were saved. The submarine that had attacked the cargo ship was the German U-486. Launched on February 12th, 1944, she left Kiel for Norway on November 6th under Oblt. Gerhard Meyer with a crew of 35 before arriving at Horten on the 9th of November for eight days of Schnorchel testing. After passing testing, she would patrol the English Channel area taking a route around the west coast of Ireland. This was Germany's prized trophy weapon.

George Bigelow would soon learn much more about this German submarine than he would ever have dreamed of. A dream that would soon turn into a nightmare.

After the long dreadful boarding process, the Leopoldville finally set sail across the English Channel. As for George, he found himself having dinner in the mess hall along with all the other men, standing in lines sometimes over 60ft long, taking over an hour to be served. Like on most of the military ships, you would be lucky to be handed a warm plate with one meat, a vegetable, a roll and potatoes creatively prepared into various dishes. With the long lines and the urgency of the cooks rushing the food from the kitchen to the mess hall, meals often arrived cold. With so many mouths to feed, men were politely reminded to talk less, eat fast and swiftly move out. As soldiers, this had already been instilled in them from the first day they set foot on a base, so following these orders was like eating cake; if only there was some!

Along with the horrible mess hall conditions, to add insult to injury, many of the latrines were malfunctioning. Now this would not have a been a huge problem if the troops were on the ground, but from the first departure many men were getting sea sick due to the Channel churning with over six foot waves.

As the last man's belly was full, the mess hall would quickly be converted into an area in which many of the men would find themselves setting up a place to sleep. In George's case, using the mess hall's stainless steel tables as miniature bunkbeds was just the trick. George would tuck his gear at the one end of the table and use his Mae West (life jacket) as his pillow to rest his head at the opposite end. There were no blankets, no sheets, no water and no pity. This is all these men had at their disposal until they reached the shores of Cherbourg. None of the over 2,000 soldiers had any thoughts that they were destined never to arrive there.

With all his gear packed away, George rested his beaten body and tired bones upon the cold steel mess hall table, exhausted from the long grueling hours of the boarding process. Only a few days ago he was in the states training to fight in a war that most men hoped would end before their number was called. Yet, to use an old cliché "in the blink of an eye," he would find himself sailing the English Channel with his rifle within arm's reach, his Mae West (life jacket) acting as a pillow comforting his head while images were exploding like camera flashes filling his mind of what this nasty war certainty had in store for him. Still, with so much death and destruction awaiting his arrival, he tried to keep only thoughts of Betty running through his mind. Betty, the most beautiful, sweetest high school girl his eyes had ever fallen upon. Betty, the girl he fell in love with, later married and who was now carrying their first child. Still, despite all the joy God had bestowed upon him, as George Bigelow laid there in the mess hall on this night, only pain and sadness consumed him. With all the physical and mental training George had endured in staying alive, there was one glaring truth he also knew; the only thing separated him from life and death was fate.

CHAPTER TEN
CHRISTMAS EVE

At around 4:30 p.m., the Brilliant reported an ASDIC contact and put out an order for the Leopoldville and other vessels to commence zigzagging, a command that had never before been given to the Leopoldville during its crossing of the channel. But due to the heavy intensity of submarine activity, crews were ordered to action stations and destroyers moved out to drop depth charges. At 1645hrs (4:45pm), with no U-boat sighted, the alert had been called off and ships were ordered to resume their previous diamond formation. Though another false alarm had been called at 1500hrs (3:00pm), it had been dismissed at 1510hrs (3:10). The convoy of ships resumed their positions in their diamond formation, with the Brilliant, Leopoldville, Cheshire, and Croix de Lorraine sailing in a straight line, and the Anthony and Hotham flanking the wing positions. This convoy of six ships was now traveling at 13 knots to the shores of Cherbourg, the crew was finally feeling some relief that they would be on land to celebrate Christmas—or so they thought.

It was now around 7pm and George was feeling his eyes getting heavy so he laid down on his cold steel bed again to go to sleep with over two hundred of his fellow soldiers. Tucking his knees up to his chest, and making space for his backpack at the end of his feet, he proceeded to set his May West under his head as best he could, securing his head and neck. With many of the lights now being turned off, George would find himself in complete stifling darkness—a cold, damp darkness like he had never experienced before.

The convoy of ships was now less than 6 miles off the shores of France. A few soldiers standing outside on the ship's deck could see the lights of the city of Cherbourg glistening in the distance. George had just finally fallen into a deep sleep, dreaming of the day when this damn war would conclude and he would be united with his wife, family and friends once again. But his dream wouldn't last long.

It was now around 7:35 when George was awakened by something so wonderful. As the majority of the over 2,223 soldiers and crew were fast asleep, George awoke abruptly for reasons that he can never know or explain to this day. Now wide awake, laying there in the darkness of the mess hall, his eyes scanned while at the same time his head tilted from side to side like the ears of a puppy zeroing in on a sound. Then he heard it! Though faint, mumbled and muffled, the sounds began to come together for him. It was the sound of men singing Christmas songs wafting down from up on the deck. At any other time, and with all the noises of the sea and the snoring of a hundred sleeping soldiers, he would not have been able to identify what was being sung. But the entire world knows the wonderful sounds of Christmas, they almost flow through our veins, and on this ominous night, with so many souls so far from home, the sweet caroling voices cut through everything like a beacon of hope.

As the men above kept singing, George found himself lying on his back, his hands folded behind his neck as a little smile appeared on his face. So many miles from home and with all the stress of sailing the English Channel to fight in the bloodiest war of mankind, something about the Christmas spirit always brings out the joy in all of us.

Laying there listening to those men singing Christmas carols, that moment on that night, nothing was going to break the spirit within George. And perhaps this is what saved him.

The man who led the group of soldiers to the outside deck singing Christmas carols was Frank Anderson, a 21-year-old lad from St. Paul, Minnesota, who had a dream of becoming an attorney. That was before his draft notice had come in the mail.

Frank, that night for whatever reason, couldn't sleep and had what he thought was this crazy idea to gather a few men to join him in going out on the deck to sing some Christmas carols. Before he knew it there were around a dozen soldiers on that deck singing their hearts and souls out.

Frank could never have dreamed that singing songs about the birth of baby Jesus would not only save his life and those with him, but change their lives forever.

CHAPTER ELEVEN
U-486

While Frank Anderson and his fellow soldiers were up on deck harmonizing Christmas carols five-and-a-half miles out from Cherbourg, a German submarine was lying submerged, waiting for a target. It was the feared U-486 with its thirty-five-man crew commanded by Gerhard Meyer that was lying in wait in the depths with one, and only one goal.

The Cheshire was following faithfully, a hundred yards behind the Leopoldville as the convoy was getting closer to the shores of France. The crewman in the crow's nest could now clearly see the lights of Cherbourg, and holding on for dear life, they watched as the waves tossed the Leopoldville and the Cheshire from side to side. Due to the stormy conditions and huge waves, even the crew of the Cheshire and the Leopoldville was ordered to stay inside and off the deck. The crewman in the crow's nest kept a lookout for German submarines at the same time gripping the narrow railing tightly to keep from being tossed into the sea. All seemed good as both troop ships were so close to land. That was until the crewman, though not sure, thought he sighted bubbles; bubbles that usually trailed a torpedo.

After seeing the torpedo's tail resembling an airplane flying under water discharging its exhaust, the crow's nest crewman could do nothing as the torpedo was heading directly towards the Leopoldville. The call went out on the radio for all hands on deck, but there was nothing the crew of the Cheshire could do but stand and watch. Watch as the German U-486 successfully launched a direct hit from a mile away to the starboard aft side of the ship. It was only a few seconds later and another torpedo was leaving its trail as it headed towards its target. Luckily, it missed both of the troop ships.

The crew of the Cheshire were in shock as smoke and flames billowed up into the darkness of the night from the direct hit to the Leopoldville. The Cheshire crew stood on deck watching as the hit had devastated compartments E-4, F-4 and G-4, flooding the compartments and blowing out the wooden staircases. These compartments were occupied by F and H Companies and the weapons platoon of E Company of the 262nd Regiment. Companies E, F and H took the brunt of the hit which completely decimated every man below. Horrible screams filled the air as fire and smoke filled the compartments. And if the screams didn't break the spirits of the helpless soldiers witnessing this devastation, the smell of burning flesh filling the air was something that no man should ever have to endure. In that short second the blast had likely taken the lives of over three hundred good men with only a handful escaping.

The crew of the Cheshire watched as many brave men on the Leopoldville risked their lives attempting to save the crew below, but there wasn't anything they could do. The flames, smoke and heat was just too intense. So most could only stand and watch as their comrades perished.

As for Frank Anderson and his fellow carolers, their Christmas spirit and their singing spared their lives that night from that German torpedo.

* * *

In the mess hall, the majority of the men were hunkered down sleeping peacefully waiting for the PA speaker to sound off and let them know they had reached the shoreline. As for George, he was laying there listening to the soldiers singing on the outside deck, attempting to make out what Christmas carols were being sung. Then out of nowhere, the sweet singing abruptly stopped, replaced by the bang of a massive explosion. Though George had never before experienced such a sound, it didn't take him long to realize that the ship had been hit by an enemy torpedo. The explosion was so powerful, it literally rocked the ship from starboard to port (right to left) to the extent that soldiers could hear metal bending and cracking all around them. Many of the rivets that secured the ship's walls and floor twisted and began to let loose. Many men were tossed across the floor as the steel mess-hall tables broke loose from the floors. Within seconds, all lights including exit lights in the mess-hall had faded to black. Now there was no light and with the ship shifting, many of the men were fighting just to stand up. Within minutes they would begin to feel the icy waters gushing in beneath them as the sea swirled around their ankles acting like an aura of death.

With the impact of the explosion, combined with total darkness, soldiers found themselves in a mad scramble to find an exit—an exit that would only be found by a stroke of luck, or by the memory of one's God-given senses.

George, after the explosion, was fortunate to still be in his bed. However, his training and military senses told him that his first move should be to quickly grab his Mae West life jacket and fasten it to his body. But there was one huge problem. In the cold darkness of the mess hall, as he reached in front of his head to take hold of his Mae West, he could feel another fellow tugging on his jacket at the same time. In the darkness he could see no face belonging to the hands at the other end of his Mae West. Not a single word was spoken or even a grunt sounded. But both men knew there was another human being at the other end of that life jacket. George, a man with more character and courage than any average man could ever have dreamed of, for a split second was caught in a tug-of-war between human sacrifice and human survival. Yet, it was his life jacket and all the men knew in case of an attack, their Mae West fastened to their bodies meant the difference between life and death in their defense against the sea. The men also knew in the severe darkness of the mess hall, if they could not find their own, chances of locating a lost one would be like finding a needle in a haystack. Not having a life jacket fastened to their backs if the ship did sink into the depths of the sea meant certain death. George and the faceless soldier tugging on the other end both knew all of this.

As George tugged on his life jacket at the same time feeling the resistance from a fellow soldier from the other end, his faith in his Lord and Savior, Jesus Christ, may have saved him from making one of the most difficult decisions any man could ever wish to make. Though the battle for the life jacket lasted for only a second or two, when George made his firm tug on the Mae West, the soldier on the other end just let go. After retrieving his jacket, George quickly fastened it to his body and instantly went into survival mode.

George would never find out who the other soldier was at the end of that life jacket that night. Nor did he ever hear if he lived. Many times through the years he wondered if maybe he should have let go first. It would be something that would linger in his soul for the remaining years of his life.

With his Mae West now securely fastened, George knew he had to quickly find the path out of the dark mess hall in hopes of making it to the upper deck. This was going to be the only way to reach the lifeboats or in the worst-case scenario an opportunity to abandon ship.

With the icy water swirling around their feet and rising fast, if fate would not allow these men to find a way out, they were only too painfully aware that certain death awaited them.

The mess hall was now totally dark and the water was rising quickly up to their knees. Though most of these proud soldiers were calm and collected, for a few, tremendous panic began to set in. However, this is where the natural born leaders of men rise to the occasion. And that's just what George Bigelow was born on this earth to be.

As staff sergeant, he kept his composure knowing his men would feed off his energy and follow his lead. He also knew the first thing he had to do was find a flashlight located in one of the storage bags and with the water rising fast, he needed to find it now! The problem for George was not finding a flashlight in a bag in total darkness, but remembering where the bag was and what bag it was in. Still, that light was going to be the difference between living and dying and leading his fellow soldiers to safety depended on his entire focus on finding that light in a bag.

TWO STRIKES AND NOT OUT

Life and religion is a funny thing at times. During all this commotion, George found time for one last prayer to his God.

In darkness and with water now passed his knees, George proceeded in the direction his intuition led him. After failing to find the bag with a flashlight during his first two searches, he frantically moved from bag to bag hoping and still praying for the bag with the light in it. In baseball terms, it began to feel like George would now have two strikes on him with only one more swing and miss before heading to the dugout. And though this was not a baseball game, George was going to keep swinging until he connected. Luckily on his third attempt, he found the bag with the flashlight. Though only one, the batteries were charged and the light was bright.

And so was George's spirit.

CHAPTER TWELVE

THE LIGHT

Troops began to flock to George who stood with flashlight now securely in hand, like the Pied Piper playing his flute. George, telling his story of this night would later say, "All the men would faithfully follow me as if I knew what I was doing, and where the hell I was going. To be truthful, with the main stairs leading to the deck blown away, I didn't have a clue which way to turn. But since I had the flashlight in my hand, the men assumed I knew what I was doing."

George shone the light back and forth methodically around the dim walls of the mess hall looking for the way out. The stream of light found the escape exit that George hoped and prayed would lead him and the men who were now seemingly in his care directly to the staircase that led to the outside deck. But as the water crept ever higher these brave men were shocked to find only the existence of a gigantic hole where the staircase once was. All that existed now was an inky blackness leading to nowhere—a place no mortal man wished to end his existence. Still, George possessed the courage to find a way out even if it meant death for himself.

The gaping hole was six to eight feet in circumference in the floor with the center resembling the dark depths of hell.

Across the hole from where the men were standing, a steel ladder hung on the wall leading to the upper deck. Whether you would call it pressure, panic, or just fear, its presence didn't change this one dreaded fact; a decision had to be made to take a running jump across the chasm to latch on to the steel bars leading them out to the upper deck. There was no other way out. The decision was easy. But the problem was that just one miscalculation in their leap to reach the other side would mean the certain peril of a fall into the abyss.

The men following George Bigelow stood behind him waiting for an answer. At the time it was an answer he didn't have.

The men standing at the edge of the gigantic hole now could hear the water rushing in down below and yet there was no response from George. He was not convinced that leaping across the black hole was the best way to survive; especially with so many men having to make the leap with so little time left to do it. Frozen in thought, George stood there for what felt like minutes, yet, only a few precious seconds had passed. Still with no word from George, a handful of men took matters into their own hands. Whether due to their courage or in their fear, a few men decided to take a running jump over the hole in the hope of grabbing on to the steel ladder at the other side.

George stood there in silence watching these courageous or maybe desperate men take their turn. One after the other, men would get the best running start they could possibly muster up and like a track star performing the long jump propelling them forward to the ladder. Still, as each man had attempted their leap, George watched as only a handful of men reached the ladder, while many more fell to their deaths. Sadly, as a man, a soldier, appointed squadron leader and keeper of the only light, he painfully endured only the guilt for not having an answer.

Then, as he stood watching one man after another disappear, suddenly his eyes opened and his senses awoke, as a sensation ran coldly through his body telling him he had no choice but to find another way out. In that moment he became single minded and completely focused. Every other feeling receded and George felt a welling up of purpose and determination. Fighting darkness and the uncertainness of each step, he took his flashlight and tiptoed his way carefully around the narrow, jagged steel edges of the hole in the floor searching for an alternate route out. Sliding one foot in front of the other making sure he and the men behind him wouldn't fall off the edges, between the smoke and darkness they blindly groped, but there was still no sign of a route leading them to safety. The desperation was palpable, the thick air was acrid and cloying, his breathing was becoming more ragged. With each step George would now take, his brain told him if something didn't appear soon—what believers would call a miracle—the only option would be to back track their steps to the front of the hole and take their chances taking the last leap to grab that elusive metal ladder for survival.

The flashlight in George's hand was a symbol of life and hope. As the black smoke swirled all around them and the cold sea water rose, he swung it back and forth searching...searching. Then, just when George's journey looked like it was over, whether it was fate or luck, a miracle appeared right in front of them.

The miracle appeared in the shape of an old steel door. And though severely mangled, this was more than just an old door but the gate to heaven for those who believed. And maybe even those who did not believe, began to. George, using his shoulder, pushed through the bent and mangled steel, creating an opening wide enough to get through. Strangely, with all the excitement about his find, it wasn't until he set foot on the other side that it really hit him, that this may be the closest to the feeling he will have before entering the gates of heaven.

As the word got back to the rest of the men, with the greatest respect for their fellow soldier and with great military discipline, one by one the men formed a line following George's lead and shouldered their way out of the grim mess hall to relative safety. Yes, George Bigelow had just saved their lives.

CHAPTER THIRTEEN
ALL HANDS ON DECK

B ut the journey was not over yet as soldiers with tremendous patience made their way from the mess hall level to the upper deck. At the same time the PA system made a loud and clear announcement, "All hands on deck, no one go below." The PA system that hadn't worked properly when it came to gathering the troops for safety drills and with most instructions in Flemish, but now the English was perfectly clear.

Upon reaching the upper deck, George could not believe his eyes, as he surveyed the destruction to the starboard side of the ship. Flames burned brightly high into the dark night sky, creating their own brooding cloud of thick smoke. If there was any doubt about the blast that had shaken the Leopoldville this night, it only took a soldier's eyes to realize it had been a direct hit from a German torpedo. Tragically, for George and the first men to arrive on deck, images of fire and smoke were quickly forgotten. It was true, their eyes bore witness to the massive destruction to the ship, but their ears for the first time heard the horrors of war, as the screams of men trapped below in the flames sent chills through those who could hear them. George and the men he had just led to safety were feeling blessed to have escaped death, but they could now only stand helplessly with their hands firmly clenching onto the cold steel railing that wrapped around the deck knowing that others hadn't been so lucky. There was nothing any of these men could do but watch and listen. Watch for life, listen for death, or maybe pray for a miracle that would never come.

There were a few men down below risking their lives in an attempt to save their fellow soldiers trapped in the burning compartments, but the flames produced such a great heat making it totally impossible for these brave men to get close.

George couldn't remember how long it was as his fellow soldiers and himself silently stood there, but he does remember it only took a few seconds for the screams to give way to silence.

As fire and smoke were still pouring from the gash in the starboard side of the ship, the men on the upper deck began to disperse realizing they needed to find safety in the life boats. For George, with so much death around him, his first thought was that he needed to find his best friend Don Goble. This was not going to be an easy task since they had been split up from the start of the boarding process. However, not seeing him on any of the starboard decks, he was going to take a chance that his buddy was located on the port side of the ship—hopefully alive!

George would make his way through the chaos of hundreds of soldiers, fighting their way to no clear destination. There was so much confusion due to the Belgian crew, including 93 Africans from the Belgian Congo, only being able to receive orders in Flemish. Even the captain on the ship, Charles Limbor, spoke no English. But these were the crew on deck with the biggest advantage to find survival, since they knew precisely the routes leading to the lifeboats and the location of any extra life jackets on the ship. With the ship's crew mostly speaking Flemish, it was almost impossible for the American soldiers to understand any instructions that were being given. That's if any instruction was ever truly given. It was unimaginable mayhem up on deck that night. Still, with so much desperation and panic all around him, George kept his thoughts focused on his goal of finding Don.

As George was attempting to find a way through to the bow of the ship, hoping to get to the port side, messages were sounding off on the loudspeaker. Though the messages were vague, George strained to hear any valuable information. The voice over the loudspeaker told the men a tug boat was on its way to tow them in; soldiers would be transferred to other boats; and the ship was not sinking. This was the exact news the men needed to hear to ease their fears. A collective sigh of relief rippled through the company. Tragically though, the loudspeaker's announcement that was supposed to act as a way to calm the men and give them confidence, was nothing more than an aberration.

After hearing the loudspeakers announcement, George, not concerned about the ship sinking now, proceeded in his journey to find his friend. But before his eyes could scan the port side deck for Don, he was taken aback by what he was witnessing. It had only been a few minutes since the loudspeaker had announced that everything was all in control with rescue boats on the way, but standing there on the deck looking down, he was shocked to see many Belgian crew members loading themselves into the lifeboats preparing for a launch away from the Leopoldville. What even made matters worse was that in the area of the ship where the lifeboats were being launched, there were some soldiers standing on top of the deck clapping, thinking these were going to be the boats that would soon lead them off the ship to the comforts of a sister ship.

At 18:25, Captain Limbor ordered all but essential crew to abandon ship. When the loudspeaker went silent, many of the soldiers were still not sure what to do or about the urgency to abandon the ship. And the mass of soldiers leaning against the deck's railing stood there watching as the ship's crew, one by one, boat by boat, sailed away—disturbingly, with no U.S. soldiers aboard.

No one ever told George, but he now knew the SS Leopoldville was truly sinking.

CHAPTER FOURTEEN
FAILED RESCUE

After Captain Limbor ordered all but essential crew to abandon ship, the U.S. soldiers still didn't panic much since the ship was still stable and not showing any signs that it was sinking. However, as the men stood on deck, left behind and watching the crew sail away to safety, they could see there were not many lifeboats aboard, and uneasiness began to set in. As for George, he had long moved on from feeling uneasy to a state of full-on survival. Pushing his way through the throng of soldiers he had not found his friend Don. He fought back the panic that Don may have succumbed to the flames or the explosion. After all, Don had become a brother to him through all the months of training, replacements for the families they had both left behind. His eyes inspected each face frantically, peering through the soot and grime to recognize Don's features, but they were all strangers.

As the Belgian crew's life boats sailed away separating themselves from the Leopoldville, George could see the ship, Brilliant, sailing towards them. History would later tell us that Captain Pringle of the Brilliant, feeling that the Leopoldville was sinking at around 18:25hrs, made a bold and risky move. He ordered the Leopoldville to drop anchor so he could come alongside. Although Captain Pringle saved over five hundred men by this maneuver, there was conjecture later that since it had taken the Leopoldville over two hours to sink, the ship could perhaps have limped to safety had she not been anchored, perhaps saving hundreds more who died needlessly in the water. At the time, no-one had any way of knowing the outcome of their decisions and this was the call he made.

With great skill and courage, he maneuvered the Brilliant

alongside the Leopoldville hoping to rescue as many U.S. men as possible. As a veteran sea captain, he was well aware that the rough seas could ram both ships against one another causing severe damage to his own ship and at the same time risking the lives of his own crew. Captain Pringle's keenness would later prove him right.

George stood at the top deck and watched, as Captain Pringle steered his ship closer and closer to the Leopoldville in an effort to provide the men with the best opportunity to leap aboard his ship. But the crashing waves tossed the two ships up and down while at the same time drawing them together and apart. Each time the two ships collided, sounds like thunder filled the air as the clashing of the ships' steel walls banging against one another sent shock waves through the feet of the men standing on the deck of the Leopoldville.

As the Brilliant positioned its way next to the Leopoldville, crewman from the Brilliant were yelling out for the men of the Leopoldville to jump aboard. Many men screamed, "Jump, it's the only way off." Ten to twenty men at a time would line up hoping to make the leap, while others waited—waited their turn, waited for another route, or maybe waited for their fear to subside.

As the two ships collided, men jumped onto the Brilliant in a state of desperation, hoping they timed their leap perfectly, as the waves pushed it closer to the Leopoldville. Standing in silence, George could hear their prayers while his eyes watched these brave men wait their turn to jump.

Though many men were successful in their attempts, many miscalculated their jumps, sadly they fell between the ships and were sucked under by the sea. However, these were considered the lucky ones since their life preservers gave them another chance for survival. Others jumped the forty feet down from the Leopoldville onto the deck of the Brilliant, landing awkwardly and breaking legs and arms in the fall. The Brilliant's crew began to throw anything they could find onto the deck to break their falls and soften their landing.

As the Brilliant maneuvered to bring itself close to the Leopoldville, the waters of the English Channel weren't so kind as the inconsistency of its waves fooled many of the men. Many men mistimed their leaps and fell between the two ships and in doing so, their bodies got crushed between the steel walls of the two ships. The sound of bones cracking and the sight of bodies falling like rag dolls into the water was like nothing any of these men had ever witnessed; nor will ever again. George clung tightly to the railing and watched in disbelief at what was unfolding before his eyes.

The Brilliant had now loaded over 500 men and with no more room aboard, Captain Pringle set sail to Cherbourg.

Captain Pringle was a hero for his courage bringing the Brilliant to save those 500 men that night. Unfortunately, his heroism was short-lived. As he passed one of the out-bound lifeboats leaving the Cherbourg shore, with no urgency, and feeling there was still ample time for the tugboats to get the remaining men off the sinking Leopoldville, he neglected to call back the escort vessels that were still in the hunt for the U-486 German submarine to return and aid in the rescue of the sinking ship. These moves would have dire consequences and prove to be a catastrophic mistake.

Captain Pringle's heroic move saving the 500 men on the Leopoldville would later be drowned out by the newspapers and horrendous public scrutiny for his many mistakes that ended up causing so many deaths.

Shockingly, in later investigations into the sinking of the Leopoldville, it was noted that Captain Limbor had radioed the Brilliant that the order to abandon ship had been given. In these proceedings, Captain Pringle stated over and over he never received the message.

Though Captain Pringle would sail the seas for another ten years, his response about never getting the message from the Leopoldville that dreadful night was never understood nor explained.

As the Brilliant pulled away from the Leopoldville, George didn't have a clue what lay ahead of him nor did he know why he never made his way to the other men who were leaping to save themselves onboard the Brilliant. But he did know he had to make some kind of move, and fast.

With no other ships in sight coming to rescue the remaining men, and not seeing his good friend Don Goble on the port side of the ship, George decided to return to the starboard side where he had begun his initial journey in the hope of finding his friend. George Bigelow had just witnessed many gruesome sights of war with all of its unspeakable fears and ghastly deaths, however, finding no sign of Don Goble, these were not the images filling his head. It's impossible to understand what causes people to act in certain ways in such unbearably stressful situations; is it family background, upbringing, schooling, army training? But standing on the deck glaring out into the darkness of the vast sea, he had no pity or fear for himself, but was only consumed by inner sadness for the loss of his friend.

Yes, it had seemed George Edward Bigelow's best friend was gone.

George realized he needed to gather himself up and find a way off the sinking Leopoldville. Unfortunately, fate was about to abruptly make this decision for him.

At around 8:40, or close to it, George heard two tremendous explosions from the bowels of the ship blowing off the hatch covers below, catapulting men off the ship and into the water. Standing on the starboard side of ship now, he gripped on to the cold iron deck rail with all his strength as the stern began to sink down, followed by the ship suddenly starting to list alarmingly to starboard.

If there would have been a gradual shifting of the Leopoldville from left to right, he may have had time to prepare, but there was no good fortune here. The ship abruptly tilted sending George off his feet, pinning him against the deck's rail. Holding on to avoid falling over the railing and into the crashing waves below, George found himself in a death-defying situation. As he desperately clutched onto the railing with all his strength, ship's debris began falling and tumbling down the floor of the deck hitting George as if he was caught in a tornado. Chairs, steel cans, wood, or whatever wasn't fastened down was now bashing against George before making its way into the sea. George could only tuck his chin into his chest, close his eyes and do his best to hold the rail as the ship's cargo furiously bruised and battered him. With every object that would strike him and with the strength in his hand weakening, thoughts flashed through his mind to just give up and let go of the rail. Although his courage did not waver, the decision of death would soon be taken out of his hands.

With time running out and George's grip fading a huge wave of water surged in without warning, banging against the side of the ship, toppling George over the deck. The torpedo had struck on the starboard side and aft, and the huge gash left by the explosion had caused the great ship to quickly become filled with water and stern-heavy. At first George thought the water was just a tremendous wave that had made its way over the starboard side of the ship, but he would soon realize that the surge of water that had overwhelmed him was not a wave at all, but the weight of the Leopoldville as she reared up almost vertically, and then was being sucked down stern-first into the sea.

George quickly found himself perilously submerged under water fighting to regain his grip on the rail, and with his breaths shortening, only unconsciousness awaited him as the listing ship sucked him into the depths of the sea. Though he fought to keep his eyes open, the sea didn't care if he could see or not, as she was now making him her own. With all his courage and fight to live, George had to come to grips with the fact that there wasn't anything more he could do but succumb to whatever God had planned for him.

So he took his last memory of Betty and his unborn son with him, closed his eyes, then let go of the rail that had been his lifeline.

As the suction of the sinking Leopoldville began to draw him down deeper and deeper to the bottom of the sea, George frantically waved his arms in an attempt to propel himself up to the surface. With only darkness surrounding him, in his fight to ascend to the surface, his body came in contact with the ship's cargo, or even worse and impossible to fathom, the bodies of some of his fellow ship mates.

While submerged in the depths of the sea unable to hold his breath any longer, he frantically opened his mouth for a split second before instantly closing it. In that fraction of a second, George knew all hope was now lost. He no longer was able to keep the water from flowing into his lungs.

As George began to sink deeper and deeper to the bottom of the sea, his arms and legs became suspended out from his body as if he was floating in space. Then all of a sudden, a vision entered his mind. It wasn't a bright white light, it wasn't the gates of heaven or even a blessing in meeting God. In the last seconds of George's life, the vision was in the form of a nine-inch TV. And in this nine-inch-screen George would find his peace.

Knowing his time on this earth was over, this nine-inch TV began to show images of his family, friends and many of his loved ones. There were his parents, and grandparents and so many people who were dear to him during his youth. As he watched the images of his life unfold it was as if time was stretched out, or suspended. Yet, as he drifted in the darkness watching this weird nine-inch screen, all that was so special to him couldn't compare to the next blessing bestowed upon him in these his last moments. As if by some miracle from God he was allowed to see into the future of his loving wife Betty and their first unborn child. You see, though Betty was three months pregnant when he left for war, there was no way of knowing whether the baby Betty was carrying was going to be a boy or a girl. Now, while he floated under the cold waters of the stormy English Channel, the nine-inch screen propitiously granted him his last blessing. With his time on Earth now running out, the screen told him that his loving wife Betty would bear a son—a beautiful boy born with the same vigor and zest for life as his father. And like his father, he would grow into a great man who cares for all and brightens up every room he steps into. And as George watched this joyous vision, he had one wish before letting himself go. George's last wish as bizarre as it may seem, was that his son would be born with beautiful curly hair. And with this, the nine-inch screen TV went blank.

Remarkably, though George would not be there to witness it, six months later his son was born with a beautiful head of curly hair.

CHAPTER FIFTEEN
FIRST STRIKE

The waters of the English Channel were very cold and George drifted into unconsciousness. By this time if George hadn't died from drowning, the 48-degree water temperature would surely kill him due to hyperthermia.

Floating to the bottom of the sea, the TV reminded him of his certainty that there would be no more Christmases, Easters or other family gatherings. He also knew the opportunity to go back and visit with many of his Lewistown friends would now be only a distant memory. But with all this hurt, nothing compared to the pain of knowing that he would never again look into those beautiful blue eyes of his loving wife Betty. To hold her, hug her and softly lay a kiss upon her lips. And when all his pain had nearly left him, his last remaining thought was that fate had cheated him out of the precious gift of holding his newborn son.

George Edward Bigelow was gone.

Sitting here writing about the life of the most impressive man that I had ever known or met, I am doing my best as I always have, not to question God, though admitting at the same time I truly do not understand Him. With that being said, It's a mystery that only God can solve why George rose out of the sea that night like a baby whale, blowing out water from his nose and mouth, while at the same time frantically grasping for any breaths of air he could take in. My confession is I certainly don't know how George came to be spared that night. Notwithstanding, if I had to guess, my guess would be the angels were not ready to take George under their wings just yet!

Reaching the surface spitting out water and gasping for oxygen, realizing he was still alive, George instinctively knew he had to attach himself onto anything floating and get out of the frigid water as best he could. Frantically spinning his head and body in circles in the hope of find anything, he noticed to his right something was moving. What it was or used to be he did not know, but reaching out in the darkness and grabbing hold, he quickly realized it was piece of wood. Not a life boat, not a life raft, just a damaged piece of lumber. Yet, grabbing onto this piece of floating lumber, he kicked and hauled himself up spluttering, propelling himself half-out of the water and onto the board. It was like a rebirth, as chaotically and frantically he grasped for survival. However, his solace in his accomplishment would not last long as within seconds he found himself next to five other men fighting to climb onto that same piece of wood; one was even a colonel.

Now with six men floating on one flimsy piece of wood, the colonel started barking out orders, "Men, get your upper bodies out of the water and hold on." Though George never knew his name, it made sense and the men starting to struggle to get their bodies up as high as possible out of the cold sea. Even so, if your upper torso was out of the water but your lower half was not, it wouldn't be long before you could become unconscious and subsequently fall off the board—and time was of the essence.

At first, George and the other men were so grateful for having found that piece of wood that was saving their lives. In this they were blessed. However, as the tide began pulling these six men away from the circles of many men still left in the water without any kind of floating device, these six men safely lying there on that precious piece of wood could only grievously look on as one by one, the men in the water fought furiously to keep from drowning. Many were thrashing around trying to find anything they could latch onto to get themselves out of the water, while others were climbing on the backs of men overcoming each other for any loose life jackets or other floating objects.

The thought of death can make the strongest man do desperate things at desperate times.

George and his fellow soldiers lay shivering in the bitter cold, their fingers numb and lips turning purple, making it almost impossible to speak; but this could not compare to the pain that was all around them.

As the six men floated there on their wooden raft they had a feeling that good fortune had fallen upon them for a second chance on life. However, that feeling was quickly overwhelmed by the cries of men screaming and begging to be saved. Many cried out to anyone who would listen while others screamed to their neighbors, others to their families, while many to their God. Knowing there was nothing they could do, for what felt like hours though minutes, these six men could only lay there and listen to their fellow soldiers' voices. The sea was filled with the sounds of pain, misery and hopelessness. Sadly, as minutes passed, the screams seemed to soften until there were no more screams at all; only silence. The cold sea, as beautiful as it may be, was now taking its place in history.

The six men floated in the water for over an hour in only silence, all around them were the bodies of their fellow soldiers who had perished. Many of the men survived the blast and even the sinking, yet with nothing to keep them out of the frigid waters, hyperthermia took its course. Many men floated past George's makeshift raft dressed as they were before the sinking of the Leopoldville; perishing in their own coats and gear.

George, though weak and now barely conscious, gazed in disbelief as each floating soldier's face told a different story. These were very young men from all parts of the country. Many were single, a few married, and some even had young kids at home. There were brothers, nephews and cousins fighting afar and alongside one another in this war of wars. Yet, with so many unique stories about these heroic men on this night, there was only one story shared by these men. They had all died for their country.

CHAPTER SIXTEEN
THE ROPE

George had no idea how long he was floating on that piece of wood that night, but with only his upper half out of the water, his body was beginning to cramp and shake due to the extreme cold as he became numb. At times he thought he may just be falling asleep, but soon realized he was really fading in and out of consciousness. With that said, his vision was still clear enough to see that the SS Leopoldville had disappeared completely into the depths of the English Channel, taking with her any remaining men aboard.

Captain Limbo would be one of those men. Feeling the guilt and the shame of letting his troops down by his own mistakes and poor judgement, Captain Limbor, taking no actions to save himself, stood at the bow as the Leopoldville sank to the bottom of the English Channel.

He would be the only officer not to survive the sinking.

Less than twelve hours ago the Leopoldville had set sail with many brave men packed together like sardines in a tin can. And now, these same men were trapped between the steel walls of the Leopoldville as it was sinking to the bottom of the sea. It was a fate no man should ever have to endure or any fellow soldier witness.

Tragically, the entire time the men were on the Leopoldville waiting to be rescued, not one man was ever instructed as to what to do if they had to jump in the water to abandon ship. For many of the men it never entered their minds how essential it was to remove any heavy coats, clothing, and boots. Due to the cold, many of the men grabbed their life jackets and strapped them on right over their winter coats without ever giving it a thought about how the weight would sink them.

A handful of men never even got the chance to survive the sea's cold waters due to something as simple as not fastening their helmets and life jackets tightly. As these men leaped off the ship's deck, upon hitting the water their life jackets and loosely strapped helmets blew up from their chest and necks, causing their heads to snap back with such force that it broke their necks. These men never even got a chance to find a board.

As George laid his head on the piece of floating wood, every crashing wave acted like an alarm clock keeping him from becoming unconsciousness. With his strength and inner will now fading to the point of no return, George laid there on his back looking into the deep blue-black night with only the glistening stars to remind him he was still alive.

Floating in the water with only a cold silence surrounding him, George's survival senses began telling him his chances of being rescued looked bleak. This was a man who had just survived the sinking of the Leopoldville, had risen out of the sea and was lucky enough to find a piece of wood to float on saving him from freezing to death. After all this, not to survive now would be the worst fate of all.

He tilted his head to his left, placed both his hands under his ear, and laid there in the fetal position just like he had as a baby. Unlike when he was under the sea, there would be no nine-inch TV now with images of home and family to sooth his soul. It was time to go to sleep and just let go. Remarkably, though thinking he was dreaming, laying there with his eyes closing and his vision becoming blurred, he thought he saw a rope floating in the water close to him. Lacking the strength to scream for help, George squeezed his eyes shut but when he opened them again the floating rope was still there, taunting him. Taking a closer look, he realized that a dream it was not, but a real rope hovering on the top of the water maybe twenty or so feet away.

For all that George knew, it was just a loose piece of discarded rope that may have fallen off the ship. His little piece of wood up to this point was his only saving grace keeping him alive. It had become his security blanket. If he chose to climb off it in an attempt to grab hold of the rope, there would likely be no way he would have the strength to swim back to it and haul himself back on it. Still, seeing his wooden vessel slowly drifting away from the rope, he had only but a few precious seconds to decide his own fate. Any man in this position would pray for a miracle, or at least to be given a sign from up above to guide him, but on this night there would be no sign. And to be fair to the man upstairs, in George's mind, he felt maybe he had already used up any miracles.

Faced with throwing his security blanket away for a rope that may lead nowhere, George decided to take a chance on that rope in the hope of meeting his maker at a later time.

So he slid off his wooden friend, said his last goodbye and with every last ounce of strength left in his body, swam to that rope.

When he reached the rope, his cold numb hands with frozen fingers reached out and firmly grabbed hold of the end. Upon securing his hold, he pulled his elbows in like a fisherman pulling in his big catch. At first there was nothing on the other end of the line, however, by the third tug George made, the line tugged back. And like an experienced fisherman, George had just reeled the biggest fish of all.

As the rope drew George in closer to the rescue ship, numerous American soldiers climbed down the rope while others leaned over the sides of the rescue boat to aid in pulling George out of the water.

Upon being pulled out of the freezing water, George was transported by the men of the rescue ship down to the boiler room, where they would prop him up mercifully against a two foot in diameter hot asbestos pipe to keep him warm. It wasn't what any hospital would likely do, but this was the only way to keep the men they pulled out of the water warm.

George had seemed to have beaten death, but that could not be said for over 700 men who never made it out of the sea alive that night. Due to the many poor judgements, communication failures and many men not working at the Fort L'Ouest base in Cherbourg because of Christmas Eve, two and a half hours had passed since the Leopoldville was struck by that German torpedo and even longer before other rescue vessels arrived.

Other rescue vessels were arriving now, but the winter darkness made it almost impossible to search for the floating men in the cold, dark sea. It was also almost impossible to tell if the men were dead or alive. Between them being unconscious and weak, for the men on the rescue boats attempting to save them it was like pulling up an anchor sunk into the sand. From there the men were transported to the docks of Cherbourg, where bodies of the men were stacked up like bags of grain as medics moved from body to body, hoping to save any man they could.

In the end, many arrived dead, many lived and a few who felt they had beaten death, died on the pier that day.

Sitting there next to that asbestos pipe fading in and out of unconsciousness and struggling to keep warm, George had no clue how long he had been in the water, how many men were saved or sadly, how many had perished. However, if that old cliché is true, "three strikes you're out," he still had two strikes left.

CHAPTER SEVENTEEN

CHERBOURG

G eorge was now safe and out of danger and finally on his way to Cherbourg on the rescue boat. He was too spent to feel relieved that he had lived through the worst experience anyone could ever imagine. He doesn't remember anything about that trip on the rescue boat and he never did find out what had happened to those other six men that night, though he did once pass the colonel who was barking out orders on their floating raft. Peculiarly, both men never said a word to each other.

The first thing George vividly remembers after arriving on shore is sitting on an old box crate with a blanket wrapped around him, watching as ambulances backed up to the rescue boats to transport the men onto stretchers. Many were fighting hyperthermia to stay alive, while others arrived with broken bones, burns and many looked paralyzed. Except for his body shutting down as a result of hours in the freezing waters, sitting there with only a blanket to comfort him, George felt God had blessed him with another chance at life, a life from this day he was never going to take for granted or waste. Sadly, when it was his turn for the medics to load him into the ambulance, his eyes saw something that instantaneously crushed all his joy at surviving that night. The sight was so powerful it immediately sent George into a deep depression, and he hasn't forgotten it to this day. As if watching the many men who died so horribly on the Leopoldville hadn't been enough that night, George looked on in horror at the pile of American soldiers stacked up one atop the other along the pier. These were brave men who risked their lives for their country, and although they were gone, stacking their bodies on top of one another like bags of grain stole one's soul.

When the ambulance pulled away, with every rotation of its tires, George hoped all the horrible memories of the sinking of the SS Leopoldville would also fade in its rearview mirror. With stretcher buckles tightly wrapped across his chest and with heavy eyes and a heavy heart George began to fall asleep. It was a sleep that for a brief time allowed him to escape from all the pain and suffering he had witnessed and endured. Shockingly when he awoke, the memories of that Christmas Eve night were not going to fade away. This night would be with him for the rest of his life.

After falling asleep, George doesn't remember much in that ambulance ride that night, but he distinctly remembers waking up in the hospital in Cherbourg the next day. This, he told me, was easy for him to remember and for good reason and although his body was battered and severely dehydrated, his eyes were in perfect working condition. So when he awoke to a nurse sitting by his side, he knew he wasn't imagining things. But as George put it, "This wasn't your typical nurse."

When George awoke in his stiff narrow hospital bed, lying next to him was the most beautiful nurse he had ever set eyes upon. George described it like this, "She had ravishing bright red hair and her eyes were as blue as the sky. Her skin was so soft and white like a Christmas snow." Then with a shy smirk he said, "Her figure was pretty good too." George would go on to tell me as he laid in his bed much too weak to move, she would take her feather soft fingers and gently dust them across his forehead and through his hair. George trying to be as honest as he can be, impressed upon me that it's hard to remember all that happened in the hospital that night seventy years ago, but he does remember one thing that has never left him. While he laid in that hospital bed with the horrible images of war unwillingly flowing through his mind, it hit him there was something much more special to this red headed beauty who rubbed his forehead and ran her fingers through his hair.

So I had to ask, "George, what made this nurse so special?"

It only took George few seconds to reply. "Larry, as beautiful as she was on the outside, she was even more beautiful on the inside." With a small tear in his eye, George ended our talk telling me, "It's hard to explain, but I felt she really cared about me and you know, I never even knew her name."

A few hours later, the Red Cross would arrive distributing new razors, shaving cream, toothpaste and other incidentals to all the men in the hospital and although it wasn't much, these small things were a blessing for a man who had just survived a German torpedo, a sinking ship and floated on a piece of wood for over two hours in the frigid waters of the English Channel. As crazy as it may sound most of us, from his favorite La-Z-Boy rocker in Florida, George told me it was the best Christmas Eve he had ever had.

CHAPTER EIGHTEEN
THE TENTS

A fter spending only a week in the hospital, most of us would assume that after what he had just been through George would get a discharge and be on his way home. But this was the war of wars and when the powers in charge sent you to fight, you fought.

A few days later all the survivors from the SS Leopoldville were transported to an abandoned horse-racing track where forty tents, each holding ten soldiers were set up as housing for the troops. Wooden planks were set up in the mud to run in front of the tents and act as sidewalks, so the men could get around more easily. On the days it rained, water and mud would at times engulf the planks overflowing into the tents, filling the floors and swamping their beds. It was January so freezing temperatures often made their way beneath their feet with a cold winter dampness filling the tents. Latrines were not plentiful and were set up at one end of the wooden boardwalk, making it a long hike for many of the men whose tent was located at the far opposite end of the camp and creating ridiculously long lines for the men waiting to do their duty. These were not the best living conditions to say the least for the many men who only a week earlier had been pulled out of the chilly waters of the bleak English Channel.

George shared with me the story of the first night he had arrived in the city of tents located in the outskirts of Cherbourg. The men were going to be treated to a post-Christmas meal since the actual Christmas meal they had been hoping for had never taken place. George described the meal as just okay since much of the food being served was the week-old leftovers that had been planned for Christmas Eve. Still, it was a special occasion sharing this meal with your fellow soldiers and giving thanks for just being alive. Yet, as George folded his hands and said his silent grace before eating, he couldn't keep away thoughts of his loving Betty. And of course, his best friend Don Goble.

After the men finished their Christmas dinner, with their stomachs bloated with many helpings of turkey and dressing, it was lights out and they made their way to their bunks. George, before dinner, had a long walk to where the cooks were serving their week-late Christmas feast that night but the good news is after filling his stomach, he had the shortest walk to the latrines since his tent was one of the first ones on the boardwalk. At least the military got something right not to serve the food in an area where the smell of human sewage would fill the air of every tent on the boardwalk. Overall it turned out to be a special night; at least for most!

It was now around midnight as George laid in his bed with arms folded behind his neck dreaming dreams of dreams, but from outside of his tent, he kept hearing a thumping noise sounding like two boards banging against one another. Not having a clue what it was, he popped up to peak out of his tent to see what the strange noise was. As he stuck his head out of his tent, the unknown thumping became very apparent. Looking down the boardwalk, George witnessed a handful of men exiting the tents in their nighties as they hurriedly were heading for the latrines. At first he was a little dumbfounded by it all, but witnessing one of the men holding his rear as he was running to the latrine, he quickly figured out what was happening.

In his own humorous way George put it like this, "Many men became sick that night and got in army language the "GI's", from that Christmas dinner." As for George, he never felt the sickly effects of that spoiled dinner that night, however, he got no sleep either due to the banging of boots all night long against the planks of the boardwalk leading to the latrines.

The tents were crowded and the food was horrible, but there was one very special thing that took place often every day. Whenever an ambulance pulled into the camp, a crowd of soldiers would gather to welcome the individual and better yet, if you were lucky you had a chance the person climbing out would be a lost friend. For George, he would never miss that ambulance opening its doors in hopes of seeing his best friend Don Goble appear, though ambulance after ambulance came and went, only shattering his hopes of ever seeing his friend.

One day George stood waiting to greet that same ambulance as he had done many times before, and yet again, to his disappointment, there was no sign of his friend. It started to become more and more apparent that each time the ambulance arrived without his friend, maybe Don Goble was no more. Saddened by the same old result, George turned to make his way back to his tent and at that very instance out of the corner of his eye he saw standing in the distance...Don Goble! Who saw who first? Neither one knew nor asked. Who spoke? neither man could remember. What only mattered was after fearing each other dead, these best friends had found each other!

As they embraced in disbelief and utter joy the tears began to flow down their cheeks and they hugged one another with a firmness that only the truest of friends could ever feel. You see, one must remember these men were more than best friends, both had watched death, felt death and beaten death while so many of their fellow soldiers had not, and now here they stood embracing each other! It was truly something so special, only they knew.

Sadly, the two would have only a few more days to savor their homecoming before they would get the call to go and grab their weapons to fight again.

CHAPTER NINETEEN
LORIENT / ST-NAZAIRE

I t had now been a week since Don and George had made their way to the boardwalk of tents pitched in a muddy racetrack, but their time there would soon be over. The famous Black Panther 66th Infantry would not be making its way to fight in the deadliest fighting at the Bulge, instead, they would be leaving to defend and contain 50,000 Germans in the Lorient/St-Nazaire regions. Whether it was due to the squadrons being vastly diminished, or the U.S. Military feeling guilty about the many failures of the SS Leopoldville disaster, reports came out many years later that it had already been decided by the powers in charge to send the more experienced 94th Division. No one ever knew but one thing was for sure, it was still a big blessing for George and Don.

It was now time for Don and George to hop into a troop transport truck and make their way south to Lorient. As the truck started pulling away, it hit them they would be leaving behind one of the most tragic events that they had ever experienced and hopefully would never experience anything like it again. This they would end up being right about, unfortunately, the memory of the sinking of the Leopoldville would fade slowly. Due to the code of wartime censorship instructing soldiers not to speak or even write home about the sinking, inaccurate reports came out for many months of missing men in action the Military felt were alive but only later it was found they were dead.

Even after the war was over, the U.S. Government was tight lipped about the events that led to the sinking of the Leopoldville and soldiers on board. Still, with all the silence, all the cover ups, the one fact they could not hide was that 763 men had perished and the many personal stories of their lives were lost with them. In the end, the SS Leopoldville has lain dead at the bottom of the English Channel for over seventy years now, evidence of a nightmare that still haunts those special remaining few even today.

Upon arriving in Lorient, George was in charge of his squadron that usually consisted of twelve men, but the Leopoldville had tragically stolen a few away. Still, with his eight or so men, he was in charge of containing and capturing any German soldiers attempting to aide German submarine pens. These pens were docking areas for submarines to get food, fuel, and troop replacement if needed and though he was outnumbered by the thousands, it was George's job to make sure this didn't happen.

CHAPTER TWENTY
DiMAGGIO

Now it was sometimes said that the soldiers who survived the sinking of the Leopoldville in a strange and bizarre way may have been spared death. This was because the Battle of the Bulge, which was their ultimate destination, a destination they never reached, became one of the bloodiest battles ever in U.S. History. 20,876 Allied soldiers died, 42,893 were wounded and over 23,554 were reported captured or missing. The Germans lost 15,652, with 41,600 wounded and 27,582 reported captured or missing. It was one of the worst examples of man killing man in modern history. For George and Don, in the five months they and their fellow US soldiers fought in Lorient containing the Germans, only 43 casualties took place in the three regiments of the 66th infantry, so one could say George and Don were really lucky, though lamentably one death is always one too many.

Since George and Don were squadron sergeants, it was their job not only to lead and make sure any new replacements were quickly educated and watched over. This not only guaranteed their safety, but the safety of the entire platoon which consisted of three squadrons.

Over the time I spent talking to George Bigelow for this book he told me many interesting and often funny stories about his experiences and the other men he served with. On one occasion when George was scanning his list of replacement soldiers, he told me he was shocked to see a name that instantly blew his mind away. Right there on his sheet was the name Joe DiMaggio! Yes! Joe DiMaggio, "New York Yankees Clipper," nicknamed 'Joltin Joe'— the professional baseball player who in 1941 hit safely in an amazing 56 straight games from May 15th through July 16th. George had read that 'Joltin Joe' had been drafted but he would never have dreamed that he would be in charge of assuring the safety of one of the greatest baseball players in history.

So with list in hand, George excitedly rushed over to the area where all the new replacements were checking in, but only having the memory of his face in the newspapers or on a baseball card to go by, he was nowhere to be found. While his eyes were still scanning the crowd, a little man standing five feet tall, if that, with a back pack twice his size strapped to his back, walked up to George and asked, "Are you George Bigelow?"

George still in the DiMaggio zone replied absent-mindedly, "Yea kid that's me."

"Mr. Bigelow, I was told to report to your squadron," he said.

George, still in the euphoria of finding *the* Joe DiMaggio, abruptly and without much patience barked out, "Your name kid?"

"DiMaggio. Joe DiMaggio."

George with a smirk answered, "Hey, kid, that's really funny. Now when you are done being a comedian, why don't you be a big help in locating the real DiMaggio." After George's request, the five-foot soldier standing in front of George stated once again, "Sir, I don't really know who you want me to be, but my name is Joe DiMaggio."

After matching up DiMaggio's papers with his own, it took a few minutes for George to take in the fact that he didn't have the real Joseph Paul DiMaggio in his squadron. Truth be told, the first word out of George's mouth when he found out he had the wrong DiMaggio was "Shit!" However, he closed out his story that day by telling me with a chuckle, "I really wasn't too upset, I never liked the New York Yankees anyway."

There were many things George had to teach little Joe, the first being an education of fox holes. Occasionally, the men could get hit with German 88s artillery. German 88s were basically short range rockets that on a calm day if you listened closely you could hear the sound of them incoming. So the men would dig these trenches around five feet deep and three to four feet wide. This was done of course so they could duck down low into the hole to avoid the enemy artillery and to take aim and return fire.

The training part was going to be a piece of cake, but the problem George would soon encounter was that DiMaggio was not just your typical short GI—he was a really, *really* short GI. He stated he was five feet tall, but looked no taller than 4'8" and that was with his boots on. George's memory told him that to even qualify to be drafted you had to be at least five feet tall, so how this little man got through the gates, on a ship and now here with him he had no clue. For a brief second George thought maybe he had some special gift or talent that the Military never told him; you know, something like a genius bomb builder, or maybe the spy of spies. Yet, if that were the case he wouldn't the hell be over here. Anyway, a major problem that George was faced with right away was that since the foxholes that were dug were over 5 foot deep, and DiMaggio being under 5 feet tall, him seeing over and climbing out was going to be a challenge!

After George had finished instructing DiMaggio about the ins and outs of foxhole etiquette, he pulled out his trusted folding chair to sit and maybe even catch a nap. But before he could close an eye, he heard the sounds of German 88s whistling through the sky.

Instantly he screamed out, "incoming 88s, hit the hole." One 88 exploded only a few yards away sending dirt and shrapnel metal over the backs of George and the other men tightly tucked in their foxholes. After the smoke cleared and it was safe to pop out, there was no sign of little Joe DiMaggio in the foxhole. George's mind was instantly filled with guilt that he may have left this little guy out there to his death. Panic stricken, he quickly began to look outside the foxhole to see if there were any signs of him. Suddenly, walking along the edge of the foxhole he saw some dirt moving inside the corner end of the hole. Though a bit confused, while peaking in closer suddenly he saw a head pop up from the dirt like a jack-in-the-box. Though it wasn't the head of anyone named Jack, it was the head of Joe DiMaggio protruding from out of the foxhole covered with ash and spitting out dirt from his mouth. George, feeling relieved that he was alive had only one question,

"DiMaggio, you ok?"

DiMaggio after spitting out the dirt cleared his throat and yelled out, "No I'm not ok and a lot of good I'm doing you. I can't see out. In fact, I can't even get out!" George and the other men did their best not to burst out laughing as DiMaggio attempted to climb out of the foxhole that day. Unfortunately for little Joe they couldn't hold back as they broke out laughing their asses off. I guess even in war one must sometimes laugh.

Joe DiMaggio did make his way out of that foxhole that day alive and all in one piece. Though he hadn't turned out to be the famous baseball player that George was anticipating on the day those replacements arrived, still, George took the same pride in getting this rookie through training camp alive and back home with his family.

I guess one could say both men hit for the cycle.

CHAPTER TWENTY-ONE

MILLARD ZUBER

In contrast to the diminutive Joe, George told me all about another of his men who was a huge, mammoth-sized man standing over 6′4″ and weighing over 250 pounds. Not only was this man big, but he had muscles on top of muscles which made some of the buttons on his shirts look like they were about to burst off. His name was Millard Zuber. Now, If there is one thing that history has taught us, it's that every team must have a practical joker who keeps everyone loose, and at times walks the tightrope line of crazy! Millard Zuber fit the above description and then some.

The file on Millard Zuber said that he had voluntarily enlisted in the Marines a couple of years earlier, but due to his unruliness, unpredictable behavior, and his uncanny big mouth, he was booted out in what the military calls a 'Dishonorable Discharge.' It didn't help either that rumor had it that he had slugged a Marine Staff Sergeant, securing his fate. Still, with the war escalating, and the United States Military needing every man it could muster up, they had drafted the misfit Zuber.

When Zuber and George first met, George, only standing 5′10″ and barely 150 pounds, was truly overwhelmed by Zuber's stature. This was one large man to say the least! When the two stood face to face to exchange pleasantries, or should I say face to chest, George's eyes were immediately drawn to Zuber's gigantic paw, as he reached out to shake hands. By comparison his own hand looked like a little doll-hand. Zuber's hand was the largest George had ever seen with its palms resembling the bottom of an oak tree stump with its limbs acting as fingers. George hesitated for a second before reaching his hand forward thinking maybe this gorilla would skip all the handshake stuff, sparing him the chance of his hand getting broken, but the aggressive Zuber reached out, took hold of George's hand and in doing so completely encompassed George's small hand like a mighty python swallowing a mouse.

Zuber knew he didn't have the edge in military rank against George but felt that what he lacked in rank he could impose in strength by squeezing this Staff Sergeant's hand until it turned blue. And that's exactly what he did. Zuber's huge paw collapsed like a vice upon George's hand hoping to get a grunt, groan or even for George to say 'shit!' However, even with George's hand losing blood circulation through it, he didn't make a peep. Instead, he stood toe to toe with this goliath of a man waiting for him to let go first. You see, Private Millard Zuber heard the stories of this man's courage and survival skills and although he was not a large man, George's courage was legendary, making him a leader amongst his men. After two seconds had passed, something had come over Zuber. He didn't really know what it was, but a transformation took place between them that would unite the men together, instead of them competing against each other.

As both men stood there with their hands tightly gripped, they saw something in one another's eyes that told them the two would become best of friends from that day forward. And that's what they became.

Now best friends, it wasn't going to change the fact that it was George's job to keep Zuber in line, but the other fact also remained; Zuber was going to be Zuber.

Zuber came into camp with some previous military experience so it didn't take any time at all for him to learn the ropes. He swiftly positioned himself as the go-to guy if one needed groceries, snacks, cigarettes and though maybe just boasting, a good woman for the night. Whether the boasting about women was true or not, Zuber, as nuts as he was, somehow always came through gaining the respect of all of his fellow soldiers. As for George, Zuber respected and loved him and the feeling was mutual.

George told me many stories about the antics of Millard Zuber, but the one that stands out was the day Zuber went fishing. As George would tell it, on the days that the men weren't on patrol or watch, they would have some free time to really do whatever they wished. For George, with a wife and baby waiting for him back in the states, he had no desire to head out to the local taverns for a drink or to make small talk with the local women. A good day for him would be the soothing relaxation of lying in his lawn chair reading a book, newspaper or just doing nothing. The majority of time sitting there with the sun caressing his face, he dreamed about the time he would be back home in the arms of his wife Betty and cuddling his newborn son who was now almost seven months old. George had only pictures of his existence. Many times laying in the chair by himself, thoughts ran through his head of a future that included birthdays, anniversaries or something as simple as a stroll through the park with Betty and his son—all the things that most of us every day take for granted.

So on this one beautiful spring day, George was taking solace in his therapeutic lawn chair. It had been a very long week and with no book in his hand, it was a perfect time to just take a long and well-deserved nap. With his heartbeat slowing and his eyelids becoming heavy, he began to fall into a deep sleep. Suddenly and without any warning, a blast sounding like German 88s exploded from the area down around the river. George immediately popped up from his chair and screamed out, "Artillery incoming, take cover." He then sprinted towards the area from which he heard the explosion to see if any of his men had been hit. Upon reaching the river, he found no 88s, no casualties and not even any of the men with a concern in the world. In fact, a couple of men were still standing at the river's bank with their fishing poles still in the water. Looking further he found a bunch of soldiers buckled over laughing their asses off. George, completely baffled for a short second, wasn't baffled for long. Seconds after his arrival, the river exploded again with the sounds of another 88 crashing its surface, heaving water and mud from the river's bottom into the air like an erupting volcano. At any other time George would instinctively have hit the dirt, but after seeing the soldiers previously laughing he clearly assessed the situation. The explosions were not German 88s, or any sort of artillery from the Germans. As a matter of fact, it wasn't even Chinese fireworks. It was disturbingly Zuber launching hand grenades into the river.

Staff Sergeant George Bigelow could not believe what he was witnessing.

Yelling at the top of his lungs he screamed out, "Zuber, what the hell are you doing?"

Zuber, with a shit-eating grin and cool as a cucumber responded, "Fishing sir."

George yelled back, "What the hell do you mean fishing?"

Zuber, standing there silently stoic, confidently just pointed to the river. George looked out at the area where Zuber directed him, and there laid dozens of fish floating on top of the water. George could only stand in silence.

Now many of you may wonder whatever happened to Zuber that day after launching those grenades into the river; the answer was nothing. George sat him down and explained to him this type of behavior cannot happen again because it will bring attention to the enemy of our location and in doing so endanger the entire platoon. George always had a way of explaining things as if he was a grade school teacher teaching first graders. Zuber respected him for this and never went fishing with grenades in the river again. And that night the three squadrons had the biggest fish fry the army had ever seen.

CHAPTER TWENTY-TWO

FRANKIE CALDERON

F rankie Calderon, like DiMaggio arrived over in France as a replacement late in the war. George never asked or knew what part of the country he came from, but he did hear some whispers he was from New Jersey. However, if he didn't know, all you had to do was listen to his talk and you knew he was from somewhere on the east coast.

Frankie was a good-looking kid and although not very tall, like most of the Europeans, he had rich black hair with olive- colored skin. George didn't know his exact nationality, although judging from his looks and demeanor his ancestors had come over from Italy or somewhere close.

One of the missions of the 1st platoon headed by George and his best friend Don Goble, squadron leader of the second, was to head out every two weeks on a patrol looking for Germans. Their objective was always the same; keep any Germans from going in and out to the shoreline pens—areas where German submarines were stationed—and on a good day they took a German prisoner. It was George's job to take them in to be interrogated. Yet, above all, the most important job for George and Don was to always secure the safety of the men in their squadron, something George really took seriously and with the utmost importance. This would turn out to be especially true for an 18-year-old rookie replacement named Frankie Calderon.

When they were on patrol looking for Germans, the method of their attack was always the same. First, a tank would lead the way clearing a path by bulldozing ahead scanning for any Germans or worse, Germans nestled down in bunkers. A bunker was the same as a U.S. fox hole except the hole wasn't as deep and the German's would pile up a higher wall of sandbags for their protection. From here there would be a small opening in which a German soldier could mount his rifle and take aim to shoot. It was a very difficult fortress to penetrate due to the opening being very small and also because a German rifleman had a machine gun unloading magazines of ammunition.

On this patrol day, the platoon met bright and early at 6 a.m. with the commander in the lead tank. Today's mission was a little more difficult since there wasn't going to be a road to drive the tank on or a path for the soldiers to walk. This mission was like many others with the tank leading the way and acting like a shield as they searched for Germans, but today the tank had the job of driving over a long stretch of hedgerow; or what we call in the States, bushes. This would be the only method of clearing the area so the men could follow the tank on foot.

The Sherman tank taking out the hedgerow for Don's squadron on the left flank and George's on the right, acted as a shield protecting the men from any frontal fire. As the tank crushed a path through the hedgerow, the protocol was for the soldiers to stay behind the tank and if the lead tank stopped for any reason, all soldiers were to kneel down with rifles aimed to kill.

One of the deadliest traits in combat that the army teaches you to conquer is the trait of complacency. Becoming too relaxed or too confident can get you and your fellow soldiers killed in an instant. This was consistently the one thing George would lecture about to the men of his squadron. Now if you were fighting in the Battle of the Bulge where bullets and heavy artillery were coming at you from all sides all the time, it's easy to stay on your toes, but the Platoons under George and Don could go for a week and not see any German fire, so it's easy to see how one could let one's guard down. Sadly, in this situation there would be no second chance to raise one's guard back up again.

It was now around the noon hour and except for the platoon working up an appetite, all seemed calm. Then about 150 or so yards out, the tank's scope spotted a few sandbags stacked up resembling a German bunker. In the countryside, Germans had constructed hundreds of these bunkers to take aim at their enemy, but many times these bunkers were merely empty holes of nothing. As the tank cautiously maneuvered its way towards the bunker, it appeared the bunker was most likely empty. Still, George with rifle up and ready, followed the tank on the left flank as he made his way towards the bunker. Then about 120 yards out from the bunker the tank suddenly stopped. George and Don both quickly ordered the squadrons to hit the ground as each soldier took their position. Except for the sound of the tank's diesel motor chugging, every man in the platoon knelt in silence with rifle butts tucked under chins and eyes acting like telescopes, they zeroed in on any movement from all direction. Suddenly, shots furiously rang out from the bunker so fast that the platoons felt it must be a surprise ambush. The platoons could only hit the ground and take aim into the German bunker while at the same time praying a bullet didn't cross their paths. As George laid on the ground exchanging fire with a shit-load of bullets flying all around his head, with no earthly way to explain it, his eyes and ears for a fraction of a second went dead. There was no sound and no movement. It was as if time stood still. Suddenly, a horrifying sound rang out to the right of him with an echo that he had never, ever heard. Not really knowing what it was, his experience and inner senses told him it wasn't good. Instantly out from the back, the panic-stricken voice of Don Goble screamed out, "Man down!" George turned his head only a notch to his right, but that's all it took to find Frankie Calderon on his back. George rushed to him screaming for a medic, but when George got to his side he knew there wasn't much he would be able to do. This youthful, inexperienced 18-year-old replacement soldier had taken a bullet directly through the front of his helmet penetrating his head. The impact of the bullet had pushed Frankie's helmet half off his head with only his chin strap keeping it still attached. George quickly knelt beside him and using his right arm he held up Frankie's head while his left hand did what a German bullet had not, removed his helmet. As George told me this story, he did his best to hold back the tears. The blood poured down his arm from the head of Frankie, and even I could feel his pain. Then he stopped telling his story, turned to me and simply said, "Larry, as I held Frankie like that in my arms, he said nothing. Judging from the massive damage the bullet had done, I knew he was gone."

Then this man of men paused once again and with water-filled eyes said, "You know, I never got a chance to say goodbye." As George and I later finished up our time that day together, George finished by telling me that for some reason he felt this young man never had a chance. I wasn't exactly sure what he meant by that statement, although, my guess was that he meant a chance to survive that bullet that day or maybe he meant just a chance to survive this crazy war with another chance for life. You know, I never asked him.

It would only be a few seconds before the medic arrived to relieve George from comforting his student. When George unwrapped his arm from Frankie's head, an inner feeling of guilt consumed him for letting Frankie down. From the first day Frankie had arrived, George took on the responsibility to do all within his power to assure this young man would make it back home. Looking down at Frankie laying there dead, George knew he had failed him. What made these feelings even more troubling for George was a strange occurrence that happened right before that fatal shot rang out. It was protocol that the Staff Sergeants would take the point leading their platoons into battle. Frankie, for some unknown reason that nobody will ever know, got himself ahead of George who was leading the point. If Frankie would have kept his proper position behind George, he likely would still be alive.

Watching the medics use all their God given gifts to perform a miracle that never came, it hit George that Frankie had taken the bullet that destiny had planned for him.

Seventy years later, the death of Frankie still haunts George.

Now one would think that the military would at least allow a little time for fellow soldiers to comfort one of their fallen soldiers, but not true. After the medic concluded Frankie was gone, noticing George was standing motionless, they ordered him to join his platoon. And that's exactly what he did.

The tank commander seeing German soldiers shooting tracer

bullets from within the bunker, sped up his tank as it made its route to intercept, as soldiers now were jogging behind the tank using it as a shield from incoming bullets. As they got closer they could see that the bunker was much larger than anticipated. Around the bunker the Germans had cleverly stacked sandbags not to tip off the numerous rifles the German soldiers had centering in on the Allied Forces. It was impossible to know exactly how many Germans were in the bunker, but it didn't take a genius to figure out there was at least one German soldier for every rifle and with the German MG-42 machine gun with a 50-250 round belt unloading its magazines of bullets, the three platoons were in for a battle.

The fighting became so fierce, the platoon had to take to the ground, taking aim at their targets from on their stomachs. As the tank made its way closer and closer to the bunker, the men would pop up, sprint to the rear of the tank, buckle down again to the ground and take their shots.

Now every platoon has a squad leader, commander or whatever title the military gives, and for good reason. In battle, you cannot have more chiefs than Indians or like the old saying, "Can't let the inmates run the prison." This was also true for the proper functions to assure the safety of all the soldiers. Yet, sometimes there are exceptions to these rules.

With tracer bullets flying through the air around George and the other three platoons like a swarm of lightning bugs on a summer June day, out of nowhere a private broke ranks from the platoon and started running past the other men laying on the ground, yelling and cussing like a possessed madman. George looked up to see what crazy soldier had a death wish, but it didn't take long to figure out who it was. Zuber was sprinting up the far-right flank with a John T. Thompson submachine gun in his hand. This was an automatic gun that could wheel off between 20-30 rounds of ammunition with one pull of the trigger. For all you gangster historians, this same machine gun would end up finding its way home to the United States but under a different name; the dreaded Tommy-Gun. It would serve as the weapon of choice for gangsters during and after the years of prohibition.

At this time in the battle total chaos had broken out with the M4 Sherman tank closing in on the German bunker. Don's squadron was running on the left flank, George's squadron on the right flank, and with the bullets, smoke and dust flying everywhere making visibility impossible, no one knew what the hell had become of Zuber.

It was impossible to see how many German soldiers occupied the bunker, but as long as the tank kept closing in and the men of the platoon were still standing and shooting, it was all good. Still, as George and Don kept moving to take aim, both were quite aware that at any time a bullet could end their friendship forever.

Finally, like the end of a bad nightmare, the tank stopped and with it the bullets. Both sides let the smoke in the air clear. George was still on one knee and had his "Bar"—Browning Automatic Rifle—locked into his armpit with his eye focused down its barrel, knowing that at any time a German could pop up firing a barrage of bullets. Yet, there was no more gunfire. Then as the skies became totally clear, from behind the top of the bunker rose a man, but it wasn't just any man. Call him courageous or call him crazy, either description would likely fit. On top of that bunker stood Zuber proudly holding his Tommy Gun in hand and sporting one of the biggest shit-eating grins that George had ever seen. Zuber had witnessed the bullet that had taken Frankie Calderon's life. In Zuber's mind, it was payback time, and the men of these three platoons were fine with that.

The commander in the tank, now feeling the coast was clear, popped open his steel hatch lid to view his victory. When George and the other squadrons got to the bunker, there were only two Germans left holding up their hands in surrender while almost forty had been killed. George told me that Zuber had likely gotten most of those.

George and Don escorted the two German prisoners out of the bunker and handed them over to the 'BAR' (Brown Automatic Rifleman) men to be taken back to the base. Then as the tank commander was just about to close his hatch, he asked George, "Are you going to take their squadrons back to camp?" George a little confuse by his questions informed him he would. That's when the commander replied, "Well you'd better get going soon." Then the commander lowered himself down below, closed his lid and his tracks spun his tank around 180 degrees to head back.

George wasn't really sure why the tank commander asked him if his men were moving forward or retreating back to the base but he was happy to see that he even gave a shit. Though all the men in this war loved and respected each other, the men in airplanes, ships and tanks had bigger egos than the majority of the men on the ground. Yet, that didn't matter to George, it was time to head back.

Seconds after George and the other men had started on their way back, the sound of artillery fire filled the air. An explosion shook the ground around the platoons before a panic-stricken voice from Goble's squadron yelled out, "Phosphorus!" as the white smoke filled the air. During this time of war, Phosphorus, or what was called WP "White Phosphorus," and had the nickname "Willie Pete" or "Willie Peter," was a chemical weapon that after exploding created a smoke and a gas that would instantaneously burn anything it came in contact with. White phosphorus was used in grenade launchers on tanks and as part of other ammunition for artillery or mortars. It didn't do well in penetrating the steel of tanks, but the capability to fiercely burn right through the thickest of clothing before melting through one's skin made it one of the deadliest weapons in the wiping out of ground troops. If one was lucky enough to survive such an explosion, the burns alone to the flesh were so catastrophic, bearing witness to them was only topped by enduring them.

After hearing the scream of phosphorus, George shouted the order for his men to stay in line and to run as fast as they could back to camp. After George had made sure all of his squadron were gathered and making their way back, around fifty feet out to his left, a soldier from Don's squadron was kneeling with both of his hands holding his stomach. Looking closer George could see that blood was oozing profusely between the soldier's fingers. Though George never saw what happened, it was obvious the wounded soldier had been hit with fragments from a WP. Upon reaching him, it became so vividly clear that the wounded soldier's hands were not large enough to cover up the horrendous opening in his stomach. Around his hands were tiny steel fragments acting like red hot coals burning through his jacket. As the medics and other men from Goble's squadron arrived, without a word and without a cry, the wounded soldier knelt there with his chin tucked into his chest looking at his hands holding his stomach. Then he slowly raised his head and scanned into the eyes of all who were there, still saying nothing. The seriousness of this soldier's injuries devastated George, but what broke George's heart was not his wound, but the look on the soldier's face that day.

The war had taught him the painful fact that many young inexperienced boys, who could not be more than 18 years old, were not going to make it home. He had already seen too many of these young boys sadly come and go. What broke him this day was not having an answer. An answer for this falling soldier whose eyes scanned into the faces of those standing around him, while holding his life in his hands, with a look on his face that begged for an answer to the question, "Why has this happened to me?" As the medics lifted the falling soldier and laid him onto the stretcher, no answer was ever given.

With the reality of war once again lying at his feet in soldier's blood, George stood motionless watching the medics depart with the wounded young boy. A million thoughts were running through his head as he stood there, before another soldier sprinted past him slapping him on the shoulder yelling, "Gotta go soldier."

George gathered himself and followed the sprinting soldier doing his best to keep up with him. George would tell me he had a hard time sprinting behind that soldier that day. He jokingly said to me "Larry, I never ran so fast in my entire life, but I must confess, even though I may have been truly the slowest man in the army, but when explosions are landing on both sides of you like the 4th of July, one runs a little faster."

George sprinted as fast as his legs would allow him to go and though he never caught up with that soldier who had tapped his shoulder, it was truly amazing that the bombs that were blowing up everything they hit, were only landing outside the left and right side of the path in which he was running. This really only meant two things; the Germans were the worst at pinpointing their launching grenade coordinates, or Don and George's platoons were the luckiest sons of bitches in the world that day.

As George got back to the camp, he was just happy to be alive. As a matter of fact, so happy, he didn't even feel all the steel fragments from an exploding bomb that had penetrated through the pants and into his left leg. The wound was not life threatening, and the medic cleaned it out as best he could, wrapping some bandages on it and sending George on his way. It was amazing with all the artillery blowing up all around them, the platoons did not lose a single man that day while dodging those bombs during their sprint back. In fact, due to the heroics of Zuber, the platoon hardly lost a man in all the gunfire during the ambush on the bunker that day. This was truly a blessing; tragically, a blessing that hadn't fallen upon that young soldier and of course, Frankie Calderon.

CHAPTER TWENTY-THREE
FRANKIE'S BROTHER

O ne day, while sitting in his La-Z-boy recliner in his condo in Florida, George began telling me there was a little more to the story about Zuber. With pen and paper in hand, laying my trusty voice recorder next to him on a coffee table, I was ready for whatever he had to give me.

Unfortunately, George must have lost his train of thought since he just sat there saying nothing. As for myself, I had a question I wanted to ask him anyway so that's just what I did. I asked "George, did you ever know what happened to that young boy who suffered that horrible wound to his stomach?" Gathering his thoughts, he responded, "Larry, strangely, I never knew if that boy lived, but judging from the tremendous hole in his stomach, I suspect he didn't." George, after telling me this, sat silently still for a few seconds as if he had taken himself back to that day. Then he looked up at me and simply said, "Now, where were we?"

I told him we were discussing the steel fragments stuck in his leg. He laughed saying again, "Oh yea, the ones that I didn't have any idea were stuck in my leg because I was running so fast in fear of getting blown up."

I replied, "Yes George, that is where we ended off." Waiting for him to begin, he once again became uncharacteristically silent. Not knowing if I should ask him if he was too tired to go on or was there something else wrong that he didn't want to tell me, I just sat there in silence waiting.

Finally, he broke his silence, 'Larry," he said, "there is one more thing I need to tell you before we move on."

"What's that George?" I asked.

He replied, "It's about Frankie Calderon." I could see in his demeanor and the tone in his voice this wasn't going to be an easy story to tell.

It was now 2006 and George was living in Bradenton, Florida when the phone rang on this day. Picking up, George almost always answered the phone the same way every time with a simple hello, a response that he never deviated from for over sixty years. Yet, on this day he told me that for some odd reason he answered this call with a, "Can I help you?"

On the other end of the phone a man's voice asked, "Is this George Bigelow?"

George replied, "Yes," again asking, "can I help you?" The man on the other end of the line then paused.

George could almost hear the caller take a deep breath before he answered, "George Bigelow, this is Anthony."

George quickly asked, "Anthony who?"

He responded, "Anthony Calderon, Frankie's Brother!"

At first George was so taken back, he took a second to pause, taking in the situation. Then he asked again just to make sure he wasn't hearing things, "Who is this again?"

The man once again replied, "Frankie Calderon's little brother." Shock had overcome George. It had been almost fifty years since the war had ended and for George the memory of that dreadful day Frankie Calderon took a bullet to his head. However, through the line of a telephone, a brother that George never knew existed would bring back that memory that he had hoped was long forgotten. Sitting there that day in George's living room, I knew this was going to be a difficult story for him to tell, yet, one which had to be told.

Many times soldiers would share with each other photos or stories of family, friends and even a girlfriend, but George never knew a single thing about Frankie's life outside the army, he never even knew that Frankie had a little brother. With that being said, the first thing George asked him was how he ever found him? Anthony said he now lived in Port St. Lucie, Florida and had found George's details through the internet. As the two shared in some small talk, the one thing George remembers is that Anthony was short on words, however, when Anthony concluded his call by asking if it would be OK for him to one day travel across the state of Florida so the two could sit and chat, George knew why. So, George and Anthony settled on a date to meet and a week later that's exactly what the two did.

George now had a week to sit and wonder what questions Frankie's little brother would likely be asking at their meeting and although not sure about many, there was no doubt about the one question Anthony would be asking—the question how did Frankie die? That was maybe the only question that George hoped he wouldn't ask.

It was January 2006 when the doorbell rang. George opened the door and there, after fifty years, stood the little brother of Frankie Calderon. Even though those fifty years had passed so fast since George had held a bullet-stricken Frankie in his arms as he left this earth, looking into the eyes of Frankie's brother, he could see a similarity between them. George enthusiastically barked out, "Come on in Anthony and take a seat."

Anthony, sat on the couch and George, in his favorite La-Z-boy. George the diplomat didn't ask or say much, he just allowed Anthony all the time to talk about his big brother Frankie. Anthony shared his deeper feelings and stories about the love and admiration he had for his oldest brother. This wasn't your typical big brother. Frankie was the big brother who had educated, taught and protected his baby brother. This was a big brother who if Anthony in his youth had had a bad dream, would wrap his arms around him and give him a hug, telling him all will be OK. This was the same big brother that on walks downtown without his parents would never let go of Anthony's hand; the brother who taught him to ride his first bike and years later how to drive his first car. Yes, this big brother was not only a brother, but in the eyes of Anthony, his idol.

Sitting there listening to Anthony tell stories of his brother Frankie, it was so obvious to George that this baby brother held his brother on a pedestal. It was a pedestal that few could ever imagine. However, with all the accolades that were flowing from the lips of

Anthony, each time George started feeling really good about these stories about Frankie, he knew the question about Frankie's death would soon be coming.

Over thirty minutes now had passed with Anthony sharing the wonderful stories of his memories of Frankie and himself during their youth. Then when George thought he may conclude this visit without discussing Frankie's death, but without any warning, all the laughter and all the smiles stopped, as words had ceased between the two. It was as if all the steam had run out of Anthony's stories but this wasn't it at all. A calmness now had settled in the room, creating an atmosphere for George to give his unrehearsed answer to a question that he really wasn't sure he knew. There were no sounds of a radio or a TV, nor any sounds from outside the front door, only the ticking sound of an old clock that hung on the wall. The atmosphere, or if you want call it the aura, created the perfect time for one of the toughest questions Anthony would ever have to ask of George and for George, well, it was of the utmost importance he had the answer.

Once the silence was broken, Anthony politely leaned over and put his left hand on George's right knee, and acting like the asking of the question was just as hard on him as it was for George to answer, with a crackle in his voice he asked, "George, how did my brother die?"

George had prepared for that question a hundred times since Anthony had called him a week ago. Yet, he still had no idea whatsoever how to describe what happened to his brother. So George took a deep breath and gazing into Anthony's eyes, he gave an answer that had never entered his mind until that second. He simply said, "Anthony, he didn't suffer."

Upon hearing this, Anthony took in his own breath, leaned back into his chair and said nothing. George reached over grabbing Anthony's arm, looked deep into his eyes and though no words really needed to be spoken, George said, "Frankie was a good man and I loved him very much. I was proud to have him in my squadron." George said no more.

George told me Anthony never asked again that day how

Frankie died, nor did he offer. Upon Anthony's departure for the door, Anthony and George embraced one another saying their goodbyes. As Anthony crossed over the door's threshold, he was not only leaving George, but the memory of the death of his big brother.

A few weeks had passed and there was never a word or even a phone call from Anthony. Then unexpectedly, a letter arrived in George's mailbox without a return address. George, though a little bewildered, didn't really care so much about where it came from as much as what was inside. He opened the envelope to find a letter from Anthony's wife. In it was a beautifully handwritten one page letter thanking George for meeting with Anthony and saying how much he enjoyed sitting down with him talking about Frankie. The letter also went on to express how their meeting had brought closure for Anthony after years of wondering if his big brother had suffered. In this, now after over fifty years had passed, he truly had found his peace.

As George read the letter, he could not keep the tears from rolling down his cheeks. Why these men's paths crossed after over fifty years is something George will never know or be able to understand, yet, it all seemed so perfect with each word written on that piece of paper that day.

When I was done interviewing George the day we spoke about Frankie Calderon, as I was leaving, he mentioned something to me that really reminded me how life sometimes works in so many mysterious ways. George turned to me and with a small tear in his eye he said, "Larry, you know I never even kept that letter Anthony's wife wrote to me. And why I didn't, I really don't know. But I wish I had."

CHAPTER TWENTY-FOUR

ARMISTICE

W ith the invasion of Germany by the Western Allies and the Soviet Union capturing Berlin, a week after the suicide of Adolf Hitler, Germany unconditionally surrendered on May 7th 1945, and Winston Churchill announced that the war was over on May 8th. This marked VE Day—Victory in Europe and the end of the Second World War. A couple of months later on July 26th 1945 the Allies would issue the Potsdam Declaration but with Japan refusing to surrender, the United States dropped atomic bombs on the Japanese cities of Hiroshima and Nagasaki on August 6th and August 9th. With the Soviet Union declaring war on Japan and the invasion of Manchuria, Japan finally surrendered on August 15th 1945 and later signed surrender documents on the deck of the USS Missouri on September 2 1945, officially ending the war.

After Germany unconditionally surrendered in early May, it was only a matter of time before the war that had taken so many lives and broken the hearts of millions would finally be over and It would be time for George to go home. However, Japan had not surrendered yet, so orders came down the pipeline for the 66th to be transferred to Marseille, France for the preparation of an invasion of Japan. George would spend his time In Marseille training the incoming men for the invasion if needed. However, after the United States dropped two atomic bombs on the Japanese cities of Hiroshima and Nagasaki, George and the other men never had to make that trip across the world through the East China Sea. Lamentably, it would take an estimated 150,000-240,000 innocent Japanese civilians dying horribly to achieve this goal.

War is truly hell.

CHAPTER TWENTY-FIVE
CLAPPY/MARSEILLE

Now with every war it's not always 24 hours of doom and gloom, but like a good ball team, you will have your share of ups and downs. However, the guys who make up that ball team, though all so different in their own special way, make up the memories that stick with you the rest of your life. This would be the case in a young green pea named Harrison.

Like in the case of most of the men in his squadron and others, George rarely knew the first name of many of the young privates since the army strictly just went by the soldier's last name. Still, no one needed a first name to make friends or at least make an assessment of who was fighting alongside you. So on the first day when Harrison and George met, George noticed the private's baby face that made him look like he was more like twelve years old than eighteen. George asked, "Private, can you tell me what your name is and where you are from?"

Feeling pressured, yet, showing George the proper respect as a higher Staff Sergeant, Harrison stood at attention and replied, "Harrison, Sir."

"Young man where are you from and how do you spell that?" George asked.

The baby faced rookie responded, "The name Harrison is a common English surname which means son of Harry, and which could also be spelled Harrisson, Haryson or Harrysson!"

Now George, being from a long ancestry of educated English descent himself, was for a split second quite impressed by this young man's answer. Although, this would soon be forgotten by the mere truth George had the greenest of green peas here and even though he may have been the brightest kid in his squadron, he was still the virgin of virgins. He also knew his self-lived experiences in the military told him these were the type of kids who stood the greatest chance of getting killed.

However, some good fate had fallen on Harrison's side since the war was coming to an end and except for the Japanese not surrendering, if this poor bastard didn't get shipped over to fight in Asia, caught in friendly fire or get himself killed by a misplaced booby trap, he was a good bet to get back home alive—maybe even better than before. While over in Europe before heading back to the states, he could visit some of his "Harrysson" English ancestry.

Well with the war ending, most of the men's spirits were at an all-time high except for the really unlucky ones whose number would be called to start packing their things to go and fight again in Japan. For George, since the army had a point system that was based on time served, married, married with kids and how many times wounded, George felt assured he would be going home. Still, he was going to give his best effort to train any of the rookies who may be heading to Asia; especially green pea Harrison.

Since George took care of most of the elements in keeping Harrison out of harm's way, he left it to the rest of the experienced troops to teach the rookies (replacements) the daily ropes of camp life. These weren't rocket-science by any means. It was more things like how far to stray off camp, what parts of the city of Marseille to keep away from, and even proper latrine ethics, etc.

One night when a bunch of soldiers got some leave time to head to downtown Marseille to knock down some beers, a small group of them came over to George's tent asking if he or any of his tent buddies wanted to join them. George didn't mind a good beer or two, but these bunch of guys had a cloudy reputation of mixing beer with a few French women and if lucky, though it didn't take luck as much as a few bucks, well you know. George being the hundred percent committed married man on these nights made it a habit to pass, with some really creative excuses. The men who knew George never challenged him, understanding his position. Although, on this night, the group swiftly skipped past George and asked the rookie if he wanted to hit the town for a good time.

George knowing the nighttime activities that go on in downtown Marseille late at night abruptly spoke up, "Fellas, Harrison just got here a couple of weeks ago, it is probably better he stay back tonight."

"Oh come on George, let the kid blow off some steam," one of the men gestured. Then the man turned to Harrison and said, "Come on kid, you want to go have some fun tonight don't you?"

Before George could say anymore, Harrison, feeling the peer pressure or maybe he really was hip to go replied, "I would love to." With that Harrison promised George he wouldn't be out too late and off he went.

George didn't have much time to sit the young naive Harrison down for some words of wisdom, but he did manage to reach out to him in an unassuming manner so as not to embarrass the lad and whispered in his ear, "Harrison, make sure you keep away from the women tonight." Harrison nodded, then eagerly joined the group of men as they welcomed him with pats on the back as they departed.

That night while George slept, he kept waking up hoping to see Harrison in his bunk, only to find it empty. The next morning fearing something had happened to him, George began searching out the guys who took Harrison out on the town hoping nothing serious had happened to him. Finally, after looking through the tents for the men who went into town last night, he came across only one of them, but after waking him, George realized the private was still stone drunk from the night before. George tried to question him about Harrison, but the private unfortunately didn't know the whereabouts of Harrison, in fact he wasn't even that sure of his own whereabouts. George kept looking for one of the other men, but it was clear to him they were either not back, or so deeply tucked in their beds with their blankets wrapped around them like mummies so as not to be disturbed. Either way, there was no sign of Harrison.

Now George or any other Staff Sergeant wouldn't give much thought of his men going out on the town one night as long as they reported for duty as designated; especially at this time when the war was officially over. However, in this case, there were two things that made George a little uncomfortable about the whereabouts of

Harrison. First, Harrison was in George's eyes the most naive, gullible and in a cute way, the most innocent boy he had ever come across in his time in the army. It wouldn't take much for this lad to get snookered or worse, mugged. The second reason for George's dismay was it may have been just three weeks prior that a private named Black with a bad habit of breaking rules, had gone into town to trade some of his personal goods for a German Luger pistol. At this time many of the U.S. soldiers were buying or bartering for these German pistols along with other German keepsakes to take home with them as souvenirs of the war. In the case of Black, on the night he went into town to find his Luger, he had never come back. And I do mean never! So obviously these thoughts were running through George's head since Harrison hadn't come home last night.

Well when all looked its bleakest, out in the distance a jeep was pulling up to the tents. There in the front seats were a couple of the guys from last night, but no signs of Harrison. Though the two looked exhausted, their spirits seemed good. With the war ending, George understood their sentiments exactly, however, an angry George approached the two men demanding from them where in the hell was Harrison. With George using his rank to get his answer, the two men just gave a bullshit look at George before their heads rolled, giving a look to the back of their jeep. There laid Harrison curled up and barely awake. The two men helped Harrison out of the back of the jeep and onto the shoulders of George as they made their way back to the tents. Doing his best to hold up Harrison, on the walk back the young private kept mumbling over and over to George, "I'm so sorry." Once inside, George helped Harrison get himself nestled in his bunk then found another blanket to keep him warm. When Harrison was now safe in the hands of George, he looked up and once again apologized to George for what he had done. George not showing an ounce of disapproval, put his hand on Harrison's arm and just told him, "Everything is good, Kid." And never spoke of it again.

Regrettably, Harrison hadn't heeded the advice George had offered him on his way out that night, and so two weeks later this youthful rookie awoke one morning with a bad case of the clap!

Yes, in the town that night Harrison became a man, but he found out it wasn't exactly worth it.

When word leaked out, which it somehow quickly did, about what had happened to Harrison, the men in his platoon and others gave him a nickname. His new name became 'Clappy.' Fortunately for Harrison, he would only have to endure this embarrassment for a few short weeks.

Upon the 40th reunion held in Washington D.C for the veterans who served in WWII, amazingly, George spotted Harrison walking down the sidewalk. One would assume after not seeing someone for forty years there could possibly be a loss for words. This wasn't the case for George. When the two men came face to face, the first word that came out of his mouth was 'Clappy!'

CHAPTER TWENTY-SIX
THE OLYMPICS

With the war now over, it was going to take a few weeks for the Military to organize the mobilization of the many of thousands of troops to get transported back to the States. So what does the Military do to keep the soldiers busy and out of trouble? Start competitive Olympics? That's exactly what Uncle Sam did.

They didn't have every sport that the real Olympics would have, but the 1940 Summer Olympics, officially known as the 'Games of the XII Olympiad' were originally scheduled to be held in Tokyo, and were cancelled due to the outbreak of the war, so this was the best they had. So the U.S. Government created the Olympic Games between the divisions in the U.S. Military and had them compete amongst each another. There was track and field, weight lifting, basketball - most of the main sports of our time.

George, being the all-American boy who loved basketball and played baseball every chance he could in his youth, would definitely find something to his liking, so he and his sidekick Don entered in archery and horseshoes! Yes, I know it sounds quirky, but that's what these two studs picked to compete in. George being totally truthful with me, one day told me, "Larry, I just loved basketball and baseball, but being such a little guy who also was as slow as molasses, I knew my career was short." So Don and George paired up and started their Olympic career shooting arrows and throwing horseshoes.

On the first day of competition in archery, things didn't really go as planned due to Don and George quickly realizing they had a small phobia of shooting arrows straight into a target. As a matter of fact, hitting the target was the least of their problem since more arrows were flying over and around the target never mind actually hitting the bullseye. Luckily for all within an arrow's distance, by the time Don and George had found the target, their career as archers was over.

Now for the average man, the embarrassment of being dismissed from the Olympic team due to a bad performance, or not to sugar coat it, a horrendous exhibition in the skill of archery, would send many packing it in, but these weren't your average men. Don and George like many others who lived and fought in WWI at this time, made up what has been called by historians 'the last great generation' and these two men were living proof of that. Not feeling at all discouraged, like the old cliché 'losers never win and winners never quit,' once they regrouped and competed in the horseshoe competition, they jockeyed their position right across the finish line.

CHAPTER TWENTY-SEVEN
PARIS FINALS

With the disappointment of archery long behind them, Don and George became so good at throwing those horseshoes, they found themselves catching a plane ride for Paris, France to compete in the Olympic Finals.

Upon arriving, the two were treated to all the best amenities the army could provide. The food was great, liquor was plentiful and believe it or not, each team had a German prisoner assigned to it to pick up the thrown horseshoes. Now many of you may feel having the German prisoners pick up the horseshoes of Americans throwing them could be construed as embarrassing or even degrading. Well this may have been true, except the German prisoners who participated in these Olympics had the same access to the same amenities as the U.S. soldiers. So you would never hear any of them complaining about picking up horseshoes.

On their first day of competition, Don and George found themselves competing against two champions from the 5th Division. This was not going to be an easy challenge since the two soldiers from the 5th Infantry were some of the toughest sons of bitches in the army, having fought in many of the battles. These two fellas had a resume that was longer than the trip across the sea. They fought on December 16th, 1944, after the Germans launched an offensive in the Ardennes forest in the Battle of the Bulge. Two days later the 5th was sent to hold down the southern flank of the Bulge, doing so successfully. Some three months later on March 22 1945, the 5th crossed the Rhine River capturing over 19,000 German soldiers. So Don and George weren't going to have a cakewalk against such well-seasoned veterans.

When the tournament contest started, all four men were battle-tested and as mentally tough as any soldier you were going to find anywhere in the Army. The only difference in these four men was one thing, the soldiers from the 5th for some reason had a style of holding the horseshoe with their fingers gripping it in the center of the ring creating an over the top rotation moving north to south when tossed. This was a completely fundamentally different method of tossing the ring than Don and George, who used what was called the "three quarter turn," where the ring is held on the end of the horseshoe and when tossed, it rotates sideways in an east to west rotation. Though at the time there was no scientific study as to which style was strategically better, one thing was for sure, a gold medal all depended on the hand of who was tossing the shoe.

As the competition between the men of the 5th and the 66th forged forward, the two sides found themselves neck and neck going into their last throws. It had now come down to the last throw and with Don holding down his position, it was all in the hands of George to put away the victory. All he had to do was get the horseshoe within a few inches from the stake, a feat that he had completed hundreds of times, and could do blindfolded. So George secured his grip on the horseshoe ring, took aim and swinging his arm back, then forward, launched the ring towards the stake. From the place where Don and George stood, the throw looked to be straight on, or what was called "dead cock on." The throw looked so good sailing through the air, even the faces of the two men from the 5th began grimacing. It was looking like Don and George would soon have a gold medal wrapped around their necks.

Well there is an old cliché that goes 'don't count your chickens until they hatch,' and this held true on this day as George's ring landed it caught a tiny corner of the ring lying in the sand previously tossed by his opponent, causing it to skip away from the stake. When George's horseshoe ring hit the sand and finally had stopped, it was so close the judges had to pull out the tape measure to see which ring was closer. George needed a toss that was within four inches from the stake, the skip had pushed him to five inches. There would be no gold medals on this today.

CHAPTER TWENTY-EIGHT

HOYT WILHELM

With the surrender of Japan, George was informed that he would be going home. Many thoughts ran through his mind. It had just been a few months ago on a cold winter night on December 24th, he was on a sinking ship that took over eight hundred men with it. How he had survived when many others had perished could only be explained as a miracle.

The orders came down the pipeline that the majority of the men stationed in Marseilles would now be transported north to Le Havre, France. Le Havre was a major port in France's northern Normandy region where the Seine River meets the English Channel. Besides being one of the largest northern ports in France, Le Havre is most famous for the heavy destruction it endured during the war. After the war, Le Havre was redesigned by Belgian architect Auguste Perret who built many landmark buildings of reinforced concrete structures, with the most famous being the iconic St. Joseph Church, with an octagonal, 107m-tall tower and a hollow center filled with illuminated stained-glass windows. The structure is truly one of Perret's masterpieces. This was all fine and dandy for the future of Le Havre, but for George and Don, they didn't care about Le Havre's past or future, the only history they cared about was that it was the city they would be sailing home from.

Once Don and George arrived in Le Havre, word had it that there may be a two to three-week period before the LST ships hit the ports to take them home. This would at times create lots of down-time with absolutely nothing to do, so many of them spent their time enthusiastically reading their mail and writing home to their loved ones about coming home.

Strangely though, George had not received a letter from Betty for the past three weeks and though he wasn't in panic mode, it was still something that very much concerned him since Betty had religiously written to him once a week throughout the entire war. There was no bad news from the rest of his family back home so George's guess was maybe just another army postal problem. Still, like many of the other men, George used this extra time to write some long and heartwarming letters to his family, friends and of course, to his beloved Betty. Sitting there writing, he was painfully aware of the many days that he had been away from Betty since the day that dreaded draft letter had arrived on March 14th, 1943. As he wrote, the memory of coming home and seeing Betty sitting all alone for hours hunched over a tear soaked kitchen table cloth was something that still breaks his heart even now. However, all this didn't matter anymore, because in a few short weeks the three would all be united together like in the most beautiful fairy tale storybook ending.

If only real life could always have a storybook ending.

One sunny day when George was standing around watching some of his buddies playing cards, a voice sounded out, loud and clear asking, "Is there anyone here who would want to play catch?" Surprisingly, with no one else volunteering, George put his hand up.

The gentleman who was asking came over and greeted George with, "Have you ever caught before?"

George not only loved and played the game of baseball as a kid, though not a big lad, was a formidable catcher in his day. So the idea of wrapping his hand in the leather of a catcher's glove again was a tremendous opportunity to show off his stuff amongst his fellow peers.

After the gentleman and George found an open field, he handed George the Rawlings web catcher's glove that had the look of having been used fairly often, though how often could that be while a war was going on, he did not know.

George's glove was your typical four finger and thumb catcher's mitt. In the 1920s, all the gloves were designed to fit only over the player's four fingers and thumb. This was until Bill Doak, a pitcher for the St. Louis Cardinals, suggested placing a web between the index finger and thumb which ingeniously gave the glove more flexibility to pinch the index and thumb together. Doak went on to patent the design before selling the rights to Rawlings. As bad luck would have it, Doak in his wildest dreams would never have guessed his design would end up being the standard in the baseball industry in gloves for the next 70 years. If he had, he would have made a boatload of money and just maybe, today's players would be wearing gloves called "Doak Gloves."

George didn't lack any confidence in catching, though it did bother him a bit when the gentleman who handed him the catcher's mitt, with a serious look on his face stated, "Good luck kid."

So after finding a nice level piece of ground, the gentleman walked off around 60 feet before leaving to find his pitcher. While George bent and stretched out his knees, he spotted a large man walking towards him and for whatever reason this man had a small entourage of men following him. The two met to exchange introductions with George politely introducing himself first, "I'm George Bigelow," and with that the large man gently reached out to shake George's hand. When both men grasped one another's hands, George could not believe the size and strength in this man's grip. It was like George sticking his hand in the mouth of an alligator and maybe as dangerous. After goliath finally let go, the man gently replied, "Hi George, I'm Hoyt Wilhelm."

Now for you people who don't follow professional baseball, Hoyt Wilhelm grew up a good old country boy in Huntersville, North Carolina and years later ended up being the best knuckleball thrower in Major League Baseball history. Nicknamed the "Old Sarge," he pitched between 1952 and 1972, winning 124 games and saving 200 games, earning him an induction into the Baseball Hall of Fame in 1985. Wilhelm entered the majors at age 30 and pitched until his retirement at age 50.

George had extreme confidence in his ability as a catcher, as a matter of fact, one would say he had "big balls" to even volunteer himself to catch the hall of famer. The problem was that this young thrower was at this time a no name pitcher in the minor leagues. So in baseball terms, George never saw what was coming. Still, with all George's confidence, when I asked him, "George, weren't you a little afraid to catch the big fella?"

He promptly responded, "No."

As George knelt into a catcher's crouch with glove in position, the big knuckleballer leaned back and let it go. Unfortunately for George, as hard as he tracked the zig zagging ball out of Holt's hand, it never touched leather. As a matter of fact, the first three or four balls almost killed him. Yet, not to be discouraged or show any signs of pressure, this little tough guy did what he had always done his entire life, after those first few misses, he stepped up catching everything Hoyt threw at him.

After George had told me the story about him feeling really good about catching this big fella, I asked, "George, come on now, you had to be a little afraid of taking a ball in the chops or worst; well you know?"

He promptly responded, "No, but my hands were scared and numb and I must confess, my buttocks were a little tight."

After Hoyt had completed his bullpen workout, the two met together just as if they were a battery completing a real Major League Baseball game. The term battery was coined by Henry Chadwick in the 1860s during the Civil war inspired by artillery batteries; on this day the term fit perfectly. When the two shook hands, Hoyt put his arm around George's shoulder and said, "Nice job rookie." It was something that George had heard many times in his life, but he had always advanced to the majors.

One final note about "Old Sarge." His career almost never had been due to the fact that while serving his country in the army, he was hit in his back and right hand by shrapnel from a German artillery explosion. Though he was awarded a purple heart for his bravery, pieces of metal remained in his hand until his death. In 2002 at the age of 79, Hoyt Wilhelm spent his last days in a nursing home in Sarasota, Florida. Who would guess that the man who offered to play catch with George some 57 years ago, lived just an hour away.

CHAPTER TWENTY-NINE
SECOND STRIKE

It was now late August in 1945 and though George had fought alongside many good men, and even saved a few, the pain of witnessing so much destruction and human loss of life only made him want to close his eyes to all of it. For every Joe DiMaggio there was a Frankie Calderon, for every Zuber there was a boy with no name holding his stomach, and through it all still, an inner guilt overcame him for surviving the war.

From the ports of Le Havre, France, George with his best friend Don Goble at his side boarded an LST ship for the voyage back to the United States. Enthusiasm filled the air as every soldier on the ship was overcome with joy to be making the voyage back home. Yet, for George and the many men who had survived that tragic night the Leopoldville sank to the bottom of the English Channel, the sea waters only brought back horrible memories. Every night George attempted to sleep, dreams that turned into nightmares plagued him of the many men who had perished. Laying there awake every night he would say a prayer that these last few days at sea would be his last reminders of the SS Leopoldville.

The ship finally arrived at a port in Baltimore, Maryland. George had only a few personal belongings such as his watch around his wrist, bag sack hanging from his shoulder, letters and of course one photograph of Betty holding their baby son, Larry. He made his way off the ship to the platform leading to the peer and then turned back to give one last look at the ship that had finally brought him home. The sinking of the SS Leopoldville was now forever behind him.

Due to the lack of army communications, George had no knowledge if anyone from home would be there to greet him. With every step on the peer George's eyes scanned the crowds in anticipation of seeing friends and family, but most of all Betty. Regrettably for him, the peer was empty. Suddenly, from way off in the distance, George heard his mother's voice screaming out loud and clear his name as she pushed through the multitude, making her way to her son. Behind his mother was his sister, Mary, struggling to keep up with her speedy mother. Colliding like freight train cars the three embraced, hugging each other like they had never done before as the tears rolled down their cheeks, merging as one. These were tears of a forgotten love for each other that had been missing these last eighteen months. It was truly one of the most blessed and joyous occasions George had ever experienced. Yet, with all the joy and blessing of seeing his mother and sister this homecoming day, sadness filled his heart; a sadness that his father hadn't made the trip with his mother and sister. He longed to hear his father say the words that told his son how proud he was that he so bravely served his country.

And of course there was Betty.

Since George had to spend a couple of days at the base before getting discharged, Ella and Mary exchanged last hugs and kisses before making their way home to Lewistown, PA. The gratitude the Army bestowed on George for doing his duty and defending his country would be a ride home in an old beat up military bus that rode so badly over bumps it made a Sherman tank feel like a Cadillac. Still, every click of the odometer signaled that George's journey was almost complete.

Upon arriving in Lewistown, Pennsylvania, George promised the taxi driver a generous tip if he put the metal to the pedal to get him swiftly home to see his wife and the nine-month-old baby that he had not even set eyes on. The driver, fully understanding George's situation, hit the gas shooting George back in his seat and went speeding away. Strangely, he never lowered the meter handle.

George's destination would not be his parent's home nor his own place of residency, but rather Betty's mother's home in the little neighboring town Reedsville. This was because at the time George had received his draft notice, the two were newlyweds and so broke it was decided it was best for Betty to go back home and live with her mother until George came back from the war. Furthermore, with Betty expecting soon, her mother would be a tremendous help with the newborn.

As the taxi drove through the countryside of Lewistown, sitting in the back seat George intently gazed out the window in anticipation of getting home. With the passing of every tree, creek and twisting road, it wasn't until he passed 'Joe the Motorists' Friend,' the place he first laid eyes on and fell in love with his prized Betty, that he realized he was really home.

With his enthusiasm of finally coming home filling the cab, he finally reached his destination. In his urgency to race out of the cab to Betty's mother's front door, reaching into his pocket for money to pay the driver he clumsily dropped his wallet to the floorboard in the cab. Furiously scrambling to pick it up while simultaneously apologizing to the driver for his mishap, George leaned forward and asked the driver what he owed him for his journey. The driver never looked back to George, then gazing into his rearview mirror and with a love-filled heart, he gave a smirk and replied, "Young man, this one is on me."

George replied, "Are you really sure? I've got it."

The taxi driver responded, "I'm absolutely sure." Pausing first for a split second to gather his thoughts, George tapped the taxi driver on the shoulder, and told him thanks. As George stepped over the curb and onto the sidewalk, the taxi driver still had not pulled away. Then from inside his cab he yelled out, "Hey kid, our country is proud of you, you take care now, OK." With a smile on his face of gratitude, George simply nodded his head.

Making his way up the sidewalk to the porch, George being George, politely knocked on the door while patiently standing waiting for his Betty to answer. It felt like minutes but it was only a few seconds, and then the door slowly opened and standing on the threshold was Betty holding in her arms the son that George had never seen until that day. Confused and overcome by emotions he didn't understand, George calmly stood looking at Betty in the doorway—a doorway that had just opened granting him his wish and uniting him with the wife he had not seen for almost two years, and the son that had only been a vision deep inside his brain. There were no words that could do it justice, no phrases that would aptly describe what George was feeling in those precious moments as he stood almost transfixed by her beauty and the overwhelming joy of meeting his son for the first time. Standing there frozen in time, his bags slipped through his clammy fingers to the porch as he moved closer gazing into Betty's face. Then ever so gently he took the palm of his right hand and with the delicateness of a feather, ran it against Betty's forehead pressing down across her cheek, and each finger that touched her face gave feeling to what had escaped him for so long. With tears flowing down both their faces, George inched closer to Betty wrapping his right arm around her and his left around his son, scooping them up and holding them tightly in his arms. At that moment it hit him his journey was finally over.

George told me he doesn't really remember how long he and Betty stood there hugging each other that day, but he does remember not many words were spoken. I guessed nothing needed to be said.

After making his way into the foyer he watched as Betty rocked their son in her arms before laying him down for his nap in an old hand-me-down baby's crib standing in a corner of her bedroom. Seeing his young wife perform such a simple task as this with their son, Larry, sent a sensation through his heart that he had never before felt. One must remember this was a father who left for war while his wife was three months pregnant and almost a year and a half later comes home to watch this beautiful picture of a mother caring for his nine-month-old son for the first time. It is true sometimes the simplest things are the most special.

After laying nine-month-old Larry down to sleep, Betty then came back into the living room taking a seat on the couch where she sat silently with her head down as she frantically rubbed the fingers of both her hands together. This was not the picture of a happy wife welcoming her husband home from war and George, concerned and maybe even a bit baffled, took his seat on the couch next to Betty. He wrapped his arm around her hesitantly and asked, "Betty, is there something wrong or something I need to know?"

George's words were hardly complete before Betty suddenly broke down and started crying profusely. Then she turned to George, reached over and passionately started hugging George with all her strength as if to say she was never going to let him break away again.

Sitting there holding his wife he didn't really know what to say or do next. Betty slowly pulled away from George's shoulder. With a crack in her voice, her words stressed to him how happy and blessed she was to finally have her husband come home after all this time. This was a big relief for George knowing nothing was seriously wrong and Betty's tears were only due to the fact that she was so overjoyed about his safe arrival home. George began to relax, everything seemed alright, while the two sat there embracing one another Betty whispered, "George, I am so sorry for behaving this way on your homecoming. I hope I didn't ruin it for you."

George responded "Betty, there is no reason to apologize for anything. I am home now and everything will be fine." Yet, as George sat there reassuring his wife that only wonderful things lay ahead in the future, he felt uneasy. Betty still seemed to be emotionally depressed. In an attempt to change the atmosphere, George asked, "Betty do you need me to do anything before your mother gets home."

Betty instantly pressed her head deep into George's chest and squeezing her fingers into his ribs she mumbled, "George, mom won't be coming home."

The words hung in the air and George, a bit confused, not quite sure what she meant, paused hoping there was more to Betty's statement, but Betty said no more. George was now dumbfounded and even a little panic- stricken, slowly and with much apprehension he asked, "What do you mean your mother is not coming home?" Lifting her head off his shoulder then pressing her lips against George's right ear Betty whispered, "Mom passed last week."

* * *

Sitting there listening to George telling me this story, spontaneously a thought came into my head; like in war not every story has a happy ending, or in George's case even a happy homecoming.

While George sat on the couch that day sharing Betty's grief at her mother's passing, his heart began breaking into little pieces seeing his Betty suffer so much pain. He could only imagine how hard the last couple of years had been for her, as a young pregnant wife with a husband away at war, and then as a young mother alone with no-one except for her own mother to help care for her newborn son. And after all of this, her mother dies.

I sat saying nothing after hearing the story about George's homecoming. Thankfully George breaking the silence turned to me and said, "Larry, I could never know or imagine the pain Betty was carrying inside of her. You know what else is very strange, looking back on it now, Betty and I never discussed her mother's death ever again after my first day back." After hearing George say this, it hit me all of us likely have things that are better off left unsaid.

Betty's story about her mother's death was sadly very tragic but what made things much worse, it came out of nowhere. At the time George and Betty got married, the parents of Betty Gilchrist were your typical American family working hard and living the American dream. For years the father owned and operated a small welding business while Mrs. Gilchrist stayed home raising the children and running the home. The Gilchrist family never missed attending Sunday mass at the Grove Memorial Methodist church each week, followed by the family sitting down for a beautifully prepared brunch by Mrs. Gilchrist. You could say the Gilchrist home was your typical happy American home.

George, sitting back in his La-Z-Boy, asked me if I remembered him telling me that Betty had written him almost every week while he was at war, but that he had become a little concerned when he had not received a letter from her for the last couple of weeks before leaving Europe for home. I mentioned that I did remember, and I curiously followed up his question with, "Did you ever know or ask why she stopped writing?"

George sat in deep thought before answering. "No, but maybe

it's because Betty was struggling with her mother's death." This is the time he went on to tell me the story behind the death of Mrs. Gilchrist.

Whether due to his memory or just his way of hiding the pain over these last seventy years, George didn't give many details or inner secrets about Betty's mother. He basically told the story that Mr. Gilchrist was a good man and a loving father who went to work every day for the past twenty-five years, came home exactly around 5pm to dinner, which Mrs. Gilchrist had prepared and symbolizing his role in the family, took his seat at the north end of the dining room table. After finishing eating, he would slip on his favorite slippers that laid next to his rocking chair, then would take a seat to watch a little TV or listen to the radio before characteristically ending his day lighting up a good cigar. George remembers about three or four months before he got home from the war, Betty wrote to say that her father was working later and later at the office to a point at times even missing the dinner her mother had prepared for him and the family every night.

Sitting on the couch that day of the homecoming, Betty now not showing much emotion and keeping her story brief, began telling George that about two months ago her father without any warning came home from work and coldly told her mother that he had fallen in love with a woman at work and would be leaving her.

While Betty told George this, she abruptly paused, waited a few seconds then with a stillness in her face and voice said, "You know George, she never even saw it coming." George, not knowing the entire details of the situation, and not helping matters was the fact that he really liked and respected Mr. Gilchrist, sat in silence.

Now Betty struggled to tell her husband about her parents but George having the gift of a good listener made it a little easier for her to explain what happened.

"The day my father announced he was leaving her," she said, "it sent my mother immediately into a deep depression. It didn't matter what I would say or do, my mother wasn't any longer the mother I once knew. It was like she was drifting away from me and I had no way of bringing her back. I was totally powerless." George

115

could not possibly imagine the pain Betty had been going through.

It had now been over two months since her father had moved out and while Betty and her younger sister did their best to manage, this once warm loving home was now only a cold wooden structure.

Sitting there in his Florida condo talking with George about what had happened so long ago, I could see so much sadness filling this 93-year-old man's face. He said this to me, "You know Larry, Betty told me her father only came back to Betty's house once after he had moved out."

I asked, "When was that George?" George became silent and still at the painful memories.

He responded, "The day that Betty found her mother dead after committing suicide."

* * *

It wasn't easy for George the first few weeks after his so-called 'homecoming day' with all the sorrow surrounding the death of Betty's mother. Whether it mattered or not, George didn't remember how Betty's mother had killed herself—maybe after seventy years that's a small blessing. But he did find a fragment of solace in knowing why his Betty had stopped writing him the last weeks of the war and of course, there was his son Larry.

All newborn children are wonderful miracles, but a first-born son is something truly special for any father and no one could be more proud and appreciative of his son.

Within a couple of weeks George and Betty found an apartment back in Lewistown where George also landed an afternoon job working for a petroleum company while Betty stayed home tending to nine-month-old Larry. With all that had happened on the day George came home, it would be an understatement to say it wasn't the homecoming he was expecting, however, George, the eternal optimist, moved full-steam ahead and immediately set the wheels in motion in achieving the goals and dreams he had planned for his family. Since he was working afternoons, his first plan of attack was to eventually go to college to become a teacher. This of course was never going to satisfy his father's dream of George becoming a doctor, as a matter of fact, it officially guaranteed the ending of the legacy of doctors going back three generations in the Bigelow family. His father in his own peculiar way never gave his blessing to George's career choice, but still, the calling to the education of children was an occupation that afforded him the opportunity to give back to society and his country; something George had already been doing rather well for a long time.

Over nine months had now passed with everything seemingly going well for the Bigelow family. Larry was growing up so fast and George, though not much, was even saving some money in the bank. Unfortunately, each time we talked, George began telling me the parts of his life that weren't going so well. His eyes would often tear up and glisten with a sadness that at times turned into hurt. And although I never asked, I began to understand why.

George did his best to explain to me that even though everything was seemingly going well with him and Betty, and that even included in the bedroom—I asked that one—he felt something just didn't feel the same as it had done before he had departed for war. George went on to say, "Maybe I didn't see it or want to admit it, but ever since my first day back, Betty was often aloof, even standoffish is a better word to describe it. Many days I would close my eyes, thinking she just needed more time due to her mother's death, but each day was the same."

I knew this was my cue to politely ask the question that I had been dying to ask and that would open Pandora's box. "George, when did Betty and you finally figure out what was bothering her?"

This man of what some still call today "The Last Great Generation," with seventy years of a hidden pain on his face said simply, "Larry, we never did fix it."

"What do you mean Betty and you didn't fix it?" I asked.

This time looking me straight in the eye, he said assertively, "You see, she came home one day and with a cold dead heart told me she wasn't happy and wanted her freedom. I guess that's all I have to say about that."

George told me that for the next month he did everything a loving husband and caring father could do in expressing his love for his wife in the hope she would change her mind. But only a few weeks after Betty had informed George she wanted her freedom, he arrived home from work one night, and as his hand reached out to turn the knob he felt a chill up his spine. His sixth sense was telling him something was horribly wrong. As he entered through the door only a cold, dark, empty house awaited him. They were gone.

During the war George had had plenty of sleepless nights, though none matched his pain on this night. Sitting alone in the darkness in his favorite reclining chair, he stared at the front door all night and into the morning in hopes Betty would enter. He imagined her apologizing and laughing it off as she explained the funny thing that happened and how she couldn't find a phone to call him. He imagined her kissing him lightly on the cheek and breezing past him into the kitchen to put the coffee on. But his heart was heavy because deep inside he *knew* and with the rising of the sun and still no sign of her, his suspicions were confirmed as he stumbled on her letter mixed in with some papers that were lying on the kitchen table.

It briefly read 'George, I am so sorry and although I still love you, I feel I must move on to find myself. I will be staying at my aunt Milly's place so please do not attempt to call or come over. I promise you I will take good care of Larry.' George folded the letter up tightly and put it in his wallet. He would go on to honor her request, never setting eyes on his once beloved Betty Bigelow ever again.

* * *

Within a month of leaving George Betty abruptly packed her belongings and moved to a small town in Kentucky where somehow, she was immediately living with an army officer on a military base! George never received word, a phone call or even a letter the day she moved south, nor did he ever have any prior knowledge of this man.

CHAPTER THIRTY

A FRIEND

A few weeks after Betty had moved to Kentucky, George received a call from his best friend in the world, Don Goble. With all that had gone horribly wrong in George's life recently, hearing Don's voice was like a miracle from heaven bringing him back to maybe not the level where he was before his departure for war, but at least now he was no longer sinking.

After Don and George were finished catching up, Don invited his best friend to pack up his things and come live with him in Hammond, Indiana so that's just what he did.

Don at this time was working at Inland Steel but there were no openings there for George, so through a good connection he got his friend a job at Sinclair Oil. George asked me if I remembered the Sinclair Oil Company that was founded by Henry F. Sinclair in 1916. I told him that indeed I did, since as a little boy I would see the large Apatosaurus, better known as Dino, dominating the gas stations' bill boards. Regrettably, I also remembered in 1969 the company was sold to ARCO, and with that sale the icon Apatosaurus and Dino became extinct.

Anyway, getting back to George, he arrived at Don's in Indiana without a car, much money and almost no personal belongings. He also now had no wife or son.

A month would go by without hearing from Betty, however, one Sunday afternoon after attending church, the phone rang at Don's home and Betty was on the other end. The call was very short and George didn't even remember what was really said, but there was one thing he did remember; after that phone call Sunday, George would never hear Betty's voice or lay eyes on her ever again. Not even the day she died. And though it seems almost impossible to fathom, ten years would pass before his son, Larry, would once again come back into his life.

Sitting on George's couch in his condo, I was hoping George would just open up and share with me why he had not seen Larry for so many years. Though I was fairly confident this wasn't going to happen, I had no idea how I should ask the question about why he had no contact with Larry for those ten years. Still, risking I may really hurt this sweetheart of a man, I gathered up just enough courage and asked, "George, I know this is a very painful subject, but I need to ask for the book. Why do you think you never kept in contact with Larry or fought for his custody?" Deep down in my soul I felt I had already found my own answer to my own question, but this was his story that needed to be told by him.

George, looking me straight in the eye and with a soft crumbling voice, mumbled, "Whether right or wrong, I just felt it was better for Larry if I stayed away."

Now I knew there was no way this proud man was ever going to tell me all his inner thoughts about those ten years without his son, but I felt compelled to express to him that I truly understood his position, hopefully releasing him from any feelings of guilt.

I asked, "George, do you ever feel maybe you have been just running away from your pain?" This was a man who had already suffered much in the war and his reward for his patriotism would be to come back home only to find his first and only love, the mother of his firstborn son, two months later runs away with another man. It doesn't take a rocket scientist to figure out something may have been a little rotten in Denmark. Still, after I offered my critique of the situation, George bravely said, "Yea, you may be right Larry. You know, I didn't really ever get a chance to know my son when I got home."

CHAPTER THIRTY-ONE
A FATHER AND A SON

Ten long years had now passed without George having any contact with his son Larry since that painful day Betty took him with her to Kentucky. And even now as I write this, it is hard for me to fathom the hurt and deep inner guilt George must have felt for not reaching out to his son. There was a story, or a rumor floating around that George's father had received an anonymous letter that Betty had separated from her husband and was frequently making the rounds at some of the local bars. Stating it in real polite terms, she was living "promiscuously."

Now George's father having many connections with the right people in the local town courts, hired an attorney and won custody of Larry. Even much more bizarrely, he did all this without giving George a heads-up as to what his plans were. Furthermore, maybe even more bizarre still, Betty, through the entire custody process, never made one phone call to George, basically letting Larry go without a fight.

All of us have different relationships with our parents and although most are wonderful, filled with beautiful memories, sadly, relationships can become stressed. In the case of James and Ella Bigelow, George loved and respected his strong dominating father very much, yet, he was probably much more like, and many times closer to his loving mother. However, the fact that his father was the dominating force in the home may explain why his mother never called George to let him know his son was now living with them.

The first day George met Larry was on one of his summer visits to see his parents in Lewistown, PA, but this visit was a little different since George's father had sent him the anonymous letter he had received in the mail a year ago about Betty's loose-living.

Yet, James Bigelow never mentioned or even hinted that he had won custody of George's son and that he had now been living with him over the last year.

Arriving at his parent's home on this hot July day, he got out of his car and walked up the steps, completely unaware that anything was different. Standing on the front porch to greet him were his parents James and Ella Bigelow, and beside them was a young boy no older than ten. With a suitcase in each hand, he made his way up to the porch, where he was greeted by his father with a simple handshake and a "Welcome home George." This was odd, since most other times he visited he didn't even get a welcome. His mother now stepped down from the top of the third step to greet her son like she had always done with the warmest and most compassionate hug. After telling her son how much she loved him and how glad she was that he was home, she took George's hand she simply said, "George, I want you to meet someone."

Then she led him to the top of the stairs and with her soft voice simply said, "George, this is your son Larry."

No mortal man could begin to explain or understand the thoughts and emotions George felt in that moment. It had been over ten long years since he had set eyes upon his son after arriving home from the war, and now here he stood. Ten years for a son to wonder who his father was and where had he gone and why. Ten years for a father to lose a son before he even saw him crawl, take his first steps or celebrate his first birthday. Ten years of praying to God he was OK with all his needs being taking care of.

As the two stood there on the porch that day, whether it was love, hurt, joy or even some guilt, neither of them really understood how to address each other, but when they both wrapped their arms around each other embracing, the two of them finally knew.

George spent almost a week with Larry and his parents that summer and in that short time, George witnessed the tremendous love and admiration Larry had for his parents, especially his father who Larry called 'Pappy.'

Whether Larry was going to stay, or leave with George had not been discussed by anyone in the family. George had his own inner feelings and thoughts of wanting Larry to leave with him, yet, due to the mistakes of the past, he found himself in the same position as when Betty ran away ten years ago. Once again, thoughts at times filled his head that Larry's life might be better if he was allowed to grow up under the nurturing of his parents. Also, Larry and Pappy had become very close over this last year, along with Ella too. George also knew that since his father had taken the initiative to bring Larry home in the first place, he would be the one pulling the strings in any decisions involving letting Larry go. If his father wanted his grandson to stay with them and not leave with his father, that's just how it was going to be. However, George's father, the rough, tough, aggressive man who always had a way of getting his way, was also a good man who took care of people when in need. And he truly loved and cared very much for young Larry.

With the entire family making their way outside to say their last goodbyes, no one in the Bigelow family still really knew what to expect from James Bigelow. This was also true of George, confused and disappointed as he started making his way to his car with a heavy heart not knowing what to expect. Then right before George reached for his car door, his father called out to him to come back. James Bigelow walked up to his son, put his hand on his shoulder and simply told him, "George, Larry's your son. He needs to be with you," and that's all that needed to be said about that.

On that day, George had finally got his son back and you know, maybe even his father too.

The years would pass quickly for George and Larry with the two becoming father and son and son and father. Regrettably, neither George nor Larry ever received a call or got even a visit from Betty over the next ten years. It wasn't until Larry was in his upper teens and living in Ann Arbor, Michigan, that he first knew the whereabouts of his mother. In his mailbox at 890 Wickfield Court was a letter from Grandma Ella Bigelow. He carefully opened it wondering what his loving grandma could have sent him. Inside the letter Larry found a clipping from the local newspaper with an obituary notice for his mother, Betty. She was 39.

Till this day, neither George nor Larry ever knew where she

was, or what she had died of. One night on February 26th, 2017, I talked to Larry on the phone and he admitted to me that she had likely died from alcohol abuse. Larry then said, "It was so very sad about my mother. You know in her early years she had a personality that lit up every room she walked into, not many people had her gift. I could see why my father loved her so and why her leaving him hurt him so much." Then he followed with, "As for me, my mother was looking to give me up for adoption before by the grace of God my grandpa came to get me. After that day, the day 'Pappy' came to pick me up, I never heard from my mother again."

In life one life can influence many lives which is perfectly demonstrated in the great Christmas movie 'It's a Wonderful Life." In the case of Betty Gilchrist, for better or even at times for the worst, I'm sure she did the best she could and in doing so had an effect on all of those around her. Case in point; at the end of my phone conversation with Larry that night, he restated to me that he felt strongly that his father loved his mother very much, and her leaving had severely hurt him. I told him I concurred. Then George's son closed with this, "Larry, let me tell you something that proves this. I believe a little in reincarnation and in saying that, my youngest of five children is my daughter Jennifer. She is this beautiful fun-loving kid that has this gift of making everyone around her feel good. When one remembers only the goodness in my mother, Jennifer is my mother's clone. Maybe it's only fate, but she is also my father's favorite."

I DON'T KNOW WHY I LOVE YOU, I JUST DO

(Epilogue)

George had just turned ninety-three years old on March 14th, 2017 which was a truly wonderful thing, but I also knew this great man wouldn't be here forever and combine that with the fact that he would soon be going back up north to Ann Arbor, Michigan, I had to get my ass going in completing his story.

On my last visit with him at his condo, with his trusty cane in hand, George walked out of his bedroom wearing his favorite brown slippers before taking his place in his Lay-Z-Boy chair. I had to hold back from laughing seeing such huge slippers at the end of his skinny legs. Looking down at these size eleven slippers, I suckered him a few times with the joke, "You know what they say about men who wear big shoes and gloves?" He never got the punch line.

This last visit was certainly going to be tough on George since the topic to be discussed would be the painful details of his first wife Betty and of course his son Larry. And although over seventy years had passed, I could feel his heart had still been deeply scarred by the relationship, making it difficult for him to talk about it. Yet, in the end, like I had said before many times, this man among men never let me down. This last interview would mark the day he got to talk about his love for the woman who had truly saved him; her name was Virginia Bigelow. To George, she was his Ginny. For me, it was my best day with him.

It was a beautiful sunny spring day in Bradenton, Florida on May 28th, 2007, but for George Edward Bigelow, this day would be the gloomiest day in his entire life. Laying in a bed on this day at a

Hospice center was the most precious lady that had ever entered his life and although she was 84 years old, the love between them was still as deep as the day both said "I do."

Also in the room that day at the hospice were his children Larry, Robin and Rebecca, and with them at his side giving comfort, George began reminiscing about his many beautiful memories of their life. A miracle had brought them together and while knowing there would be no miracle on this day, as he stood gazing into the face of this wonderful lady that had always been there to catch him when he fell, he realized she had saved him in ways he could never have imagined.

George was in his early twenty's when he and best friend Don Goble, back from the war and living in Hammond, Indiana were struggling with the concept of dating. It had been two long years since George had kept company with a woman, and he wasn't sure even how to go about meeting anyone. Striking out at a few bars was humbling, but it still wasn't nearly as bad as landing a date then later wishing you had never stepped up to the plate; in any circumstance, these two so-called studs were in a slump and a new game plan was severely needed.

After a couple of rough weeks, Don had come up with this ingenious idea to start attending a few Sunday Masses in the area in the hopes of finding some good-looking women. As crazy as it sounded, Don's theory was quite rational; churches had many more women in one location to evaluate, and how wrong can a guy go dating a Christian girl?

With the plan not working so well at a couple of Catholic churches, through a suggestion from a friend of a friend, Don and George found themselves attending First Church of the Nazarene which was right up the street from their apartment in Hammond, Indiana.

Entering through the church doors Don and George always felt some guilt knowing what their true intentions were for being there, but after quickly conquering their consciences, which by the way didn't take very long, the two found themselves sitting in the last pew behaving like two young altar boys.

Now these two Romeo's didn't lack anything when it came to personal charm or staying cool, but it was quite a different story when it came to attending a church of a different denomination. As practicing Methodists their entire lives, the two looked a little ridiculous when attempting to read unfamiliar scripture readings and singing church hymns they had never rehearsed. However, this minor challenge quickly vanished when in the very front of the church stood some of the most beautiful young women Don and George had ever seen. Making things even more enlightening, there had to be at least a half-dozen of them to pick from.

Up on the stage of the church choir was a variety of ladies; there were tall ones, short ones, thin ones, heavy ones, blondes, brunets, red heads and although many looked gorgeous and sang incredibly, one voice stood out amongst the rest. Instantly taken back by this girl's wonderful voice and her extreme beauty as well, Don sensing fate had finally shifted his way in the search for the girl of his dreams exuberantly turned to his best friend George to point her out. But as he did, something abruptly stopped him dead in his tracks. Standing there as still as a statue in a daze was his lifelong friend with his eyes totally fixated on the same girl. Now this was not uncommon for himself or George to find the same girl to be attractive, but something just seemed different this time. As Don stood there looking at his best friend, there was a twinkle in his eye that he had never seen before for any women. And although Don wasn't really sure what George saw in this girl that day that instantly mesmerized him, seeing a glow radiating from George's face told him after all that his dear friend had been through, it was his turn.

After church was finally over and parishioners were clearing, with the courage of a tiger and balls of an elephant, the two studs sneaked their way towards the choir section. As they reached the front pew, they saw the girl who had literally sent George into a self-induced coma standing there. From the tip of her toes to the top of her head she was perfect. She wore a beautiful soft pink dress with glowing white slippers on her feet that would have made Cinderella envious. Her rich brown eyes matched her reddish hair that, due to a birth mark, had an accent of white across her forehead. And although Don had relinquished this gorgeous lady, as the old cliché goes "what goes around comes around," because standing next to George's princess was a girlfriend that spontaneously caught Don's fancy! Don didn't know at this time that the girlfriend would end up being his soul mate until the day he died.

After George and Don were finished introducing themselves, using all the charm they could muster up, the two politely asked if they would be interested in going out on a double date together. Now since the time was 1948, a good night on the town would be a movie then later a stop at the local malt shop for a hamburger and a shake. However, when George and Don asked what these girls would like to do, their response wasn't as simple as going to the malt shop for a milkshake. These two young ladies not only were good looking but also much likely sharper than Don and George. They threw a curveball at them by asking, "Have you two gentlemen ever played tennis?"

With Don never having played tennis a single day in his entire life starting to stutter before answering, in risking blowing their golden opportunity with these two girls for a night out on the town, George abruptly hopped in to save the day.

Unfortunately for George, he was no better off than Don since not only had he never actually held a racket in his hand, but while growing up he always felt only sissy's played tennis. Even so, playing tennis or not playing tennis, George with his ambition in connecting with this girl calmly and with tremendous confidence replied, "Sure we have."

Upon hearing this, the young choir girls responded back "Great, after church next week we all get together and hit some balls." And a week later that's exactly just what the four of them did. Regrettably for George and Don, just not very well.

After that first meeting in a church pew, a few weeks later the four found themselves not only dating but also becoming the best of friends themselves over the next fifty years. It was almost like both of their lives mirrored one another as the two young ladies shared an apartment together and even teaching at the same elementary school together. George and Don also roomed together and though didn't work side by side, the two almost spent their entire waking moments together when not at work. Their close friendship led to hundreds of nights double dating with never having a single squabble between them; creating a bond that most of us in this world could only dream of.

Within a year both would choose each other as their best man and maid of honor in each other's weddings creating a bond for over the next fifty years until one by one left this earth.

When it came time for George to ask this girl to marry him, the job wasn't going to be an easy one since her father was a Pastor of the Church of the Nazarene in Bradley, Illinois. George had a huge hill to climb in full-filling the shoes of her father, however, up to the task the two got married and that same day headed to Hot Springs Arkansas for their honeymoon.

A small ceremony set for a few friends and family, the day became even more special when his brother Fred drove their mother cross country from Lewistown PA for the wedding, unfortunately, the day wasn't completely perfect. So, as it was at George's high school graduation, his father was a no-show.

With the years passing by like the four seasons, George and his bride found themselves in Evanston, Illinois where he worked as a live-in property keeper while at the same time enrolling at Northwestern University. He would later obtain a BA in Business Education, however, the job he remembers best was at Wieboldt's department store selling women's shoes. Here he not only became an expert on every style of women's shoe sold in the country, but also learned a few good lessons about salesmanship in the selling of shoes to boot; pardon my expression.

The first lesson George learned early was since salesmen were paid on the number of shoes sold, no matter how awful a shoe may look on the customer's foot, if the customer felt it looked great on her foot, totally agree with her and quickly box them up. The second lesson without trying to sound too cruel, if a customer comes in with a bad limp or using a cane, since time is money and money is time, pass them on to the rookie salesman because those people usually take forever to buy a pair of shoes. And without passing judgement, the third and most important lesson of all, if a very, very large customer comes in and sits down wearing a short dress, go hide in the back.

After his graduation from Northwestern University, they eventually made their way north up I-94 to Ann Arbor, Michigan where his wife found a job teaching music in a local grade school while at the same time he landed a teaching job at Tappan Junior High and later at Pioneer High School. There he taught business and of all things, typing. Now although typing was only at the time an elective course, George still had some real cool kids still attending his class looking for an easy 'A'. One example of this was the year he had college-professional football player and coach-great Jim Harbaugh in his class, and although Jim was an outstanding student, the day came when George had to call Jim Sr. about his son consistently being late to class. Jim Sr. a football legend himself, upon receiving the phone call about his son's tardiness—well, let's just say his son was late no more.

Also, walking the halls of Pioneer High School was another famous person and although George never had him in his class, he would grow up to be one of the greatest rock and roll singer-songwriters in the world, the legendary Bob Seeger who later formed the Silver Bullet Band.

By the time George was in his thirties life had brought him three wonderful children in Larry, Robin and Rebecca and like their parents, all three grew up very successful but more importantly, all three always gave back more than they received.

Thirty years had now passed and with all their children all married and with kids of their own, retirement was at George's feet. Picking a place to retire became easy due to the Missus having at times serious asthma attacks causing difficulty in her breathing. So they purchased a small condo in Bradenton, Florida where they spent the rest of their life playing golf, swimming, dancing and singing at the club house talent shows and doing what the two loved most of all; traveling the world whenever and wherever their hearts desired. I guess some could say George and the love of his life lived an almost perfect life.

* * *

It had now moved to a second day in 2007 in the Hospice and his love, Ginny, would spend it in a soft sleep, but the few times she did open her eyes, George could still see them glistening like stars in a deep blue night sky. Each time she opened her beautiful eyes he would take her hand and her touch felt as soft as the tip of a feather; but this is not why he loved her so. It was her deep inner beauty and the love she passed on to all she touched that made her so very special. Yes, destiny had brought marriage, three wonderful children and total love and commitment that had lasted for over sixty years. However, life on this earth was now coming to an end and it was time for George to say goodbye.

Sitting there listening to him talk about his second wife, Virginia, on this last day, maybe due to the fact that I was on the last chapter in my long journey with him, I found myself much more calm than I had ever been before. Maybe I was so relaxed because as I sat there on his flowered couch like so many times before with the matching pictures of flamingos staring at us from his walls, I had never seen him so happy. It was as if he had waited patiently for these pages to get written about his 93-year-old life so he could now finally talk about his Ginny.

Before Ginny entered his life, George was at his lowest point with Betty leaving him and taking Larry, but God sent Ginny to save him and that's exactly what she did. In time she not only became his wife and the mother of his children, she never stopped being his best friend.

At this point in this little two bedroom condo where George was sharing his most significant moment in his entire life with me, whether due to him telling the story or me hearing it, an aura filled the air drawing us both inside that Hospice room that day and although I was baffled by it all, I would soon find out why.

Sitting in his chair like he had done each time I interviewed him, he gave me the ending to my book.

George told me after he had laid next to his Ginny whispering to her, his internal spirit told him it was time for him to sing to her their favorite song 'I Don't Know Why (I Just Do).' After finishing singing to Ginny, he left her side and sat in his chair. Their daughter, Rebecca, was now standing over her mother and within only a few seconds after her father finished his song, she looked at her mother, then turned to her father and said, "Dad, Mom is gone."

George told me he felt that Ginny had waited that day for him to say his last good bye, and of course sing to her their favorite song. And who can argue with that.

After listening to George finish telling his story, without warning, George spontaneously began singing the song word for word, verse for verse just as he had done that day lying next to Ginny on her death-bed, concluding when he could no longer remember the words.

I could only sit there in amazement as this man sang this song about the love he had for his wife as if he was still lying next to her.

When George was finished singing his song, although I had a few more questions written down in my notebook to be asked, holding back my tears, I simply turned to him and said "George, I think that's all for today." I then got up, gave him my typical hug before heading for the door.

After leaving George that day, upon arriving home I immediately wrote down the song he sang to me and started researching it on my computer. The words were from the 1933 popular song written by Fred E. Albert with lyrics by Roy Turk 'I Don't Know Why (I Just Do)'. Looking back at that day when George sang to me his wife's farewell song, I can honestly say it touched me in ways that even today I cannot explain, yet there is one thing I did understand; The story of George Edward Bigelow (the greatest man that I had ever known) was now complete.

THE END

Top left
PFC Lawrence Harrison
Top right George

Bottom left
PFC Frankie Calderon

Bottom right picture: Top left - Zuber, Top right - George
Bottom left - Borlin, Bottom right - Harrison

On previous page:

Top Row
left - Betty
center - George, Barry, Harrison (back row)
Zuber (front row)
right - Zuber

Middle Row
left - Lawrence Harrison
center - Zuber, Bigelow (back row)
Borlin, Harrison (front row)
right - Borlin and Calderone

Bottom Row
left - Calderone
center - Calderone
right - Wm. Barry

Betty and son Larry

Top row, Juanita (L) and Lisa (R)
Bottom row, Larry (L) and George (R)

IN MEMORY OF THOSE LEOPOLDVILLE SURVIVORS WHO SUBSEQUENTLY
LOST THEIR LIVES DURING OPERATIONS AGAINST GERMAN FORCES IN
BRITTANY, NORTHWEST FRANCE, IN THE VICINITY OF LORIENT AND
SAINT-NAZAIRE. THEIR SELFLESS SACRIFICE AND VALIANT EFFORTS TO
RESTORE FREEDOM AND LIBERTY TO THE PEOPLE OF THE REPUBLIC OF
FRANCE STAND AS AN EXAMPLE TO FREE MEN EVERYWHERE, AND WILL
LONG BE REMEMBERED.

KANSAS
S/SGT MORTON E. MAGIE   CO.C 264TH INF

PENNSYLVANIA
PFC NICK PALUMBO   CO. E 264TH INF

MINNESOTA
PFC BURNETT B. JANCHER   CO. B, 264TH INF

TENNESSEE
PFC JAMES L. BLACK   CO. B. 264TH INF

STATE UNKNOWN
2LT JOHN D. MCARTHUR CO. F, 262ND INF

George on the vessel navigating his way
to the site where the Leopoldville sank

Hoyt Wilhelm

George meeting with former student/University
of Michigan football coach Jim Harbaugh

Virginia Ruth Bigeli

February 19, 1923 – May 28, 2007

Made in the USA
Columbia, SC
09 April 2018